THIS CHANGES EVERYTHING

OCCUPY WALL STREET
and the 99% MOVEMENT

Edited by Sarah van Gelder
and the staff of *YES! Magazine*

BK

Berrett–Koehler Publishers, Inc.
San Francisco
a BK Currents book

Berrett-Koehler Publishers, Inc. 235 Montgomery Street, Suite 650, San Francisco, CA 94104-2916, Tel: (415) 288-0260; Fax (415)362-2512; www.bkconnection.com

ORDERING INFORMATION

QUANTITY SALES. Special discounts are available on quantity purchases by corporations, associations, and others. For details, contact the "Special Sales Department" at 235 Montgomery Street, Suite 650, San Francisco, CA 941040-2916. Quantity discounts are also available from YES! *Magazine*: (206) 842-0216 or www.yesmagazine.org/OWSbook.

INDIVIDUAL SALES. Berrett-Koehler publications are available through most bookstores. They can also be ordered directly from Berrett-Koehler: Tel: (800) 929-2929; Fax: (802) 864-7626; www.bkconnection.com. This book may also be ordered from YES! *Magazine*: (206) 842-0216 or www.yesmagazine.org/OWSbook.

ORDERS FOR COLLEGE TEXTBOOK/COURSE ADOPTION USE. Please contact Berrett-Koehler: Tel: (800) 929-2929; Fax: (802) 864-7626.

ORDERS BY U.S. TRADE BOOKSTORES AND WHOLESALERS. Please contact Ingram Publisher Services, Tel: (800) 509-4887; Fax: (800) 838-1149; E-mail: customer.service@ingrampublisherservices.com; or visit www.ingrampublisherservices.com/customers/howtoorder.aspx for details about electronic ordering.

Berrett-Koehler and the BK logo are registered trademarks of Berrett-Koehler Publishers, Inc.

Printed in the United States of America

Berrett-Koehler books are printed on long-lasting, acid-free paper. When it is available, we choose paper that has been manufactured by environmentally responsible processes. These may include using trees grown in sustainable forests, incorporating recycled paper, minimizing chlorine in bleaching, or recycling the energy produced at the paper mill.

Cataloging in publication is available from the Library of Congress.

ISBN 978-1-60994-587-9

Cover design by Kelly Shea, assisted by Tracy Loeffelholz Dunn
Interior design by Kelly Shea, based on a template by Valerie Brewster
Copyediting on selected articles by James Trimarco
Proofreading by Samantha Schuller
Cover photo by Kurt Christensen
Part I photo (page 14) by Brett Casper
Part II photo (page 50) by Fran Korten
Part III photo (page 68) by Brett Casper

This book is dedicated to the occupiers of Zuccotti Park, who challenged the Wall Street system on behalf of all of us, and to the thousands of people in other Occupy sites across the United States and the world. Your commitment to nonviolence, solidarity, justice, and a better world for the 99% has truly changed everything.

—the staff members of *YES! Magazine*
and Berrett-Koehler Publishers

Royalties from the sale of this book will go to support the Occupy Wall Street/99% movement; five hundred copies of the book will be distributed at no charge to Occupy sites.

CONTENTS

FOREWORD

FRAN KORTEN

Late on Friday, October 7, 2011, I received an e-mail that set me on fire. It was from Steve Piersanti, president of Berrett-Koehler Publishers. He asked if YES! *Magazine* would be interested in publishing an "instant book" on Occupy Wall Street.

Since our founding in 1996, YES! *Magazine* has explored alternatives to corporate domination. We've covered efforts to create food justice, reform health care, build local economies, and solve the climate crisis. Our board chair (my husband), David Korten, has inspired us with deep insights on how to transform our economy. But time and again we've seen powerful interests associated with the 1% stop the needed changes.

So when a small group of activists began camping out in a park just blocks from Wall Street, we took notice. YES! editors Brooke Jarvis and Christa Hillstrom started posting articles on the movement. Steve commented that our coverage was the most thoughtful he had seen.

We were immediately taken with Steve's idea of doing a book—and producing it fast. We found most media reports on the Occupy movement confusing or dismissive. By producing a book now we felt we could help the growing number of people interested in this movement understand its import. Staff at Berrett-Koehler, which has published many books on themes related to the movement, felt the same way.

Sarah van Gelder, executive editor of YES!, quickly assembled articles to 1) feature voices from inside and outside the movement, 2) spotlight changes capable of shifting our society's wealth back to the 99%, and 3) show the power of social movements to bring about change. And then the production marathon began.

We decided to write in a voice that recognized that we, too, are part of the 99%. Staff members were spending time at Occupy Seattle. Susan Gleason and Sara Kirk were shipping copies of the "New Livelihoods" issue of YES! to Occupy groups. Sarah van Gelder was interviewed about the movement on PBS NewsHour. Staff were eager to donate book royalties to the movement. Berrett-Koehler offered five hundred copies of the book to distribute to Occupy sites.

We are grateful to the authors and photographers for their quick responses. At *YES!* Kelly Shea with help from Tracy Dunn designed the book. James Trimarco (who was on the ground in Zuccotti Park) provided valuable edits. Jessica Lind-Diamond, Christa Hillstrom, Derek Hoshiko, Rebecca Nyamidie, Ayla Harbin, Idil Levitas, Jennifer Kaye, Kate Malongowski, Melinda Monroe, Connie Walton, Julie Katana, and Doug Pibel edited content and assured its accuracy. Samantha Schuller did final proofreading. Sharon Booth produced marketing copy. The *YES! Magazine* editorial team—Doug Pibel, Madeline Ostrander, Valerie Schloredt, and Tracy Dunn—produced our fifteenth anniversary edition on schedule despite the extra demands of this book. All the while, *YES!* staff and interns kept our programs running, including Rod Arakaki, Audrey Watson, Gretchen Wolf, Jing Fong, Michael Winter, Paula Murphy, Bridget McCarthy, and Neil Cresswell.

At Berrett-Koehler, Steve Piersanti provided wise guidance and unflagging enthusiasm on a daily basis. His colleagues were a dream to work with. Mike Crowley, Dianne Platner, Rick Wilson, Jeevan Sivasubramaniam, Kristen Frantz, Katie Sheehan, Cynthia Shannon, Marina Cook, Zoe Mackey, Courtney Schonfeld, David Marshall, Bonnie Kaufman, Johanna Vondeling, and other BK staff supported the design and production work, helped prepare and disseminate marketing materials, and arranged distribution through many different channels.

I am deeply grateful for the millions who are dedicated to transforming our societies to benefit the 99%. And I feel blessed to work with a remarkable team so ready to bring forth a positive vision of the possibilities that lie ahead.

Bainbridge Island, Washington
October 31, 2011

Fran Korten is the publisher of YES! Magazine.

INTRODUCTION:

HOW OCCUPY WALL STREET CHANGES EVERYTHING

SARAH VAN GELDER

> "We fail to understand why we should have to pay the costs of the crisis, while its instigators continue to post record profits. We're sick and tired of one injustice after another. We want human dignity back again.
>
> This isn't the kind of world we want to live in, and it's we who have to decide what world we do want. We know we can change it, and we're having a great time going about it."
>
> *From #HowToCamp by the Spanish* indignados, *whose occupations in cities throughout Spain helped inspire Occupy Wall Street*

Something happened in September 2011 so unexpected that no politician or pundit saw it coming.

Inspired by the Arab Spring and uprisings in Europe, sparked by a challenge from *Adbusters* magazine to show up at Wall Street on September 17 and "bring a tent," and encouraged by veteran New York activists, a few thousand people gathered in the financial district of New York City. At the end of the day, some of them set up camp in Zuccotti Park and started what became a national—and now international—movement.

The Occupy movement, as it has come to be called, named the source of the crises of our time: Wall Street banks, big corporations, and others among the 1% are claiming the world's wealth for themselves at the expense of the 99% and having their way with our governments. This is a truth that political insiders and the media had avoided, even while the assets of the top 1% reached levels not seen since the 1920s. But now that this genie is out of the bottle, it can't easily be put back in.

Without offices, paid staff, or a bank account, Occupy Wall Street quickly spread beyond New York. People gathered in Boston, Chicago, Los Angeles, Portland, Atlanta, San Diego, and hundreds of other cities around the United States and claimed the right of *we the people* to create a world that works for the 99%. In a matter of weeks, the occupations and protests had spread worldwide, to over 1,500 cities, from Madrid to Cape Town and from Buenos Aires to Hong Kong, involving hundreds of thousands of people.

The Occupy Wall Street movement is not just demanding change. It is also transforming how we, the 99%, see ourselves. The shame many of us felt when we couldn't find a job, pay down our debts, or keep our home is being replaced by a political awakening. Millions now recognize that we are not to blame for a weak economy, for a subprime mortgage meltdown, or for a tax system that favors the wealthy but bankrupts the government. The 99% are coming to see that we are collateral damage in an all-out effort by the super-rich to get even richer.

Now that we see the issue clearly—and now that we see how many others are in the same boat—we can envision a new role for ourselves. We will no longer be isolated and powerless. We can hold vigils all night when necessary and nonviolently face down police. We are the vast majority of the population and, once we get active, we cannot be ignored. Our leaders will not fix things for us; we'll have to do that ourselves. We'll have to make the decisions, too. And we'll have to take care of one another—provide the food, shelter, protection, and support needed to make it through long occupations, bad weather, and the hard work of finding consensus when we disagree.

By naming the issue, the movement has changed the political discourse. No longer can the interests of the 99% be ignored. The movement has unleashed the political power of millions and issued an open invitation to everyone to be part of creating a new world.

Historians may look back at September 2011 as the time when the 99% awoke, named our crisis, and faced the reality that none of our leaders are going to solve it. This is the moment when we realized we would have to act for ourselves.

The truth is out: The system is rigged in favor of the wealthy

One of the signs at the Occupy Seattle protest reads: "Dear 1%. We were asleep. Now we've woken up. Signed, the 99%."

This sign captures the feeling of many in the Occupy movement. We are seeing our ways of life, our aspirations, and our security slip away—not because we have been lazy or undisciplined, or lacked intelligence and motivation, but because the wealthiest among us have rigged the system to enhance their own power and wealth at the expense of everyone else.

Critics of the movement say they oppose the redistribution of wealth on principle. But redistribution is exactly what has been happening for decades. Today's economy redistributes wealth from the poor and middle class to those at the top. The income of the top 1% grew 275 percent between 1979 and 2007, according to the Congressional Budget Office. For those in the bottom 20 percent, income grew just 18 percent during those twenty-eight years.

The government actively facilitates this concentration of wealth through tax breaks for corporations and the wealthy, and bailouts for giant banks and corporations. These entities also benefit from mining rights, logging rights, airwave rights, and countless other licenses to use common assets for private profit. Corporations shift the costs of environmental damage to the public and pocket the profits. Taxpayers bear the risk of global financial speculation while the payoffs go to those most effective at gaming the system. Instead of investing profits to provide jobs and produce needed goods and services, the 1% put their wealth into mergers, acquisitions, and more speculation.

The list of government interventions on behalf of the 1% goes on and on: Tax breaks favor the wealthy, global trade agreements encourage offshoring jobs, agricultural subsidies favor agribusiness over family farms, corporate media get sanctioned monopolies while independent media gets squeezed

The people who go to work producing things we need—the middle class and working poor—pay the price for all this. Speculative profits act as a drain on the economy—like a hidden tax. They are one of many reasons the middle-class standard of living has been slipping.

This lopsided division of wealth corrupts government. Few among the 99% now believe government works for their benefit—and for good reason. With the 1% commanding an army of lobbyists and doling out money from multimillion-dollar campaign war chests, government has become a source of protection and subsidies for Wall Street. No wonder there isn't enough money left over for education, repairing roads and bridges, taking care of veterans and retirees, much less for the critical transition we need to make to a clean energy future.

The system is broken in so many ways that it's dizzying to try to name them all. This is part of the reason why the Occupy movement hasn't created a list of demands. The problem is everywhere and looks different from every point of view. The one thing the protestors all seem to agree on is that the middle-class way of life is moving out of reach. Talk to people at any of the Occupy sites and you'll hear stories of people who play by the rules, work long hours, study hard, and then find only low-wage jobs, often without health care coverage or prospects for a secure future.

And many can find no job at all. In the United States, twenty-five million people are unemployed, underemployed or have given up looking for work. Forty-five percent of those without jobs have been unemployed for more than twenty-seven weeks. Some employers won't hire anyone who is currently unemployed. Meanwhile, the cost of health care, education, rent, food, and energy continues to rise; the only thing that's falling is the value of homes and retirement funds.

Behind these statistics are real people. Since the Occupy movement began, some who identify themselves as part of the 99% have been posting their stories at wearethe99percent.tumblr.com. Here's one: "I am a lucky one. I have enough money to eat three of four weeks of the month. I have been paying student loans for fifteen years and still no dent. My husband lost his job...Last year I took a 10 percent pay cut to 'do my share' and keep layoffs at bay. I lost my house. I went bankrupt. I still am paying over one thousand dollars in student loans for myself and my husband and that is just interest. We will not have children. How could we when we can't even feed ourselves? I am the 99%."

Another personal story, by a sixty-year-old, reads, "Got laid off. Moved two thousand miles for new job. Pays 40 percent less than old job. Sold home at a loss. Filed Chapter Eleven. Owe IRS fifty thousand dollars. Fifteen thousand dollar per year debt for son's tuition at state university. Seventy-five percent of retirement funds shifted to the 1%! I am the 99%!"

The Web site contains thousands of stories like these.

Now that we know we are not alone, we are less likely to blame ourselves when things are hard. And now that we are seeing the ways the system is rigged against us, we can join with others to demand changes that will allow everyone to thrive.

We the people now know that we have the right, and the power

The power of the Occupy Wall Street movement is rippling out far beyond the people camped at Zuccotti Park in lower Manhattan, and even beyond the occupation sites springing up in cities around the world. This movement is reaching people who are carrying a protest sign for the first time, including some conservatives, along with union members who have been fighting a losing battle to maintain their standard of living.

Hundreds of thousands have participated in the protests and occupations, millions support the occupations, and tens of millions more support their key issues. Polls show that jobs continues to be the issue that most concerns us, yet the national dialogue has been dominated by obsession with debt. While just 27 percent of Americans responding to an October 2011 *Time Magazine* poll held a favorable view of the Tea Party, for example, 54 percent held a favorable view of the Occupy Wall Street movement. Of those familiar with the protests, large majorities share their concerns: 86 percent agreed that Wall Street and lobbyists have too much power in Washington, DC, 68 percent thought the rich should pay more taxes, and 79 percent believe the gap between rich and poor has grown too large.

The movement has been criticized for its diversity of people and grievances, but in that diversity lies its strength. Among the 99% are recent graduates and veterans who can't find work, elderly who fear losing their pensions, the long-term unemployed, the homeless, peace activists, people with a day job in a corporate office who show up after work, members of the military, and off-duty police. Those involved cannot be pigeonholed. They are as diverse as the people of this country and this world.

The movement has also been criticized for its failure to issue a list of demands. In fact, it is easy to see what the movement is demanding: quite simply, a world that works for the 99%. The hand-lettered protest signs show the range of concerns: excessive student debt; banks that took taxpayer bailouts, then refused to help homeowners stay in their homes; cuts in government funding for essential services; Federal Reserve policies; the lack of jobs.

A list of specific demands would make it easier to manage, criticize, co-opt, and divide the movement. Instead, Occupy Wall Street is setting its own agenda on its own terms and developing consensus statements at its own pace. It's doing this in spaces that it controls—some in parks and other public spaces, others in union halls, libraries, churches, and community centers. On the Internet, the movement issues statements and calls to action through Twitter, Facebook, and its own Web sites. From the start it was clear that the movement would not rely on a mainstream media corrupted by corporate interests.

The Occupy Wall Street movement does not treat power as something to request—something that others can either grant or withhold. *We the people* are the sovereigns under the Constitution. The Occupy Wall Street movement has become a space where a multitude of leaders are learning to work together, think independently, and to define the world we want to live in.

Those leaders will be stirring things up for years to come.

This Is What Horizontal Power Looks Like

When political parties talk about building a base, they usually mean developing foot soldiers who will help candidates win election and then go home to let the elected officials make the decisions. The Occupy Wall Street movement turns that idea on its head. The ordinary people who have chosen to be part of this movement are the ones who debate the issues, determine strategies, and lead the work.

Working groups take care of practical matters like food, sanitation, media, meeting facilitation, and receiving packages from supporters. Other groups discuss the issues, create arts and culture, debate tactics, and consider whether to issue demands. In Zuccotti Park, the Consciousness Working Group set up a permanent sacred space for prayer and meditation;

spiritual leaders from various faiths show up to lead observanc-
es. The early weeks of the occupation coincided with Yom Kip-
pur, and a thousand Jewish activists participated in services
across from Zuccotti Park. They erected in the park a *sukkah*, a
temporary hut built to represent the impromptu housing Isra-
elites used in the desert when escaping Egypt. Because the
building of structures at Zuccotti Park is forbidden, this was an
act of civil disobedience.

At the center of this movement are general assemblies,
where decisions are made by consensus. Facilitators are
charged with managing the process so that all have a chance to
be heard and everyone has a chance to express approval, disap-
proval, or to block consensus by means of hand signals.

The use of the people's microphone is a central feature of
the general assemblies. To use the people's mic, a person first
grabs the attention of the crowd by shouting, "Mic check!"
Then, he or she begins to speak, saying a few words at a time,
so that others can shout the words on to those behind them in
the crowd.

Originally developed as a way to circumvent bans on amplification at many occupation sites, the people's mic has developed into much more than that. It encourages deeper listening
because audience members must actively repeat the language
of the speaker. It encourages consensus because hearing one-
self repeat a point of view one doesn't agree with has a way of
opening one's mind. And it provides a great example of how
community organizing works best when it's people-powered
and resilient. This technique allows crowds of thousands to
communicate, and also allows groups involved in direct street
action to make democratic decisions on the fly.

The occupation zones are not just places to talk about a new
society. They are becoming twenty-four-hour-a-day experiments
in egalitarian living. Without paid staff or hierarchies, everyone
gets fed, laundry gets done by the truckload, disagreements get

facilitated, and those arrested are greeted by crowds of cheering supporters when they get out of jail.

Cynics might question the importance of this deepening sense of community. But people who have lived in a competitive, isolating world are tasting a way of life built on support and inclusion, in some cases for the first time. They are sharing the risk of police beatings, arrests, and pepper spray, and the hardship of sleepless nights in a rainy or snowy park. The resulting bonds create strength, solidarity, and resolve. Visitors report being surprised to see smiles instead of anger. This is a movement where you often hear the words, "I love you."

That experience of community is not easily forgotten, and it deepens the yearning for a new culture; one that is radically inclusive, respectful, supportive, and horizontal.

What Next?

The organizers of the September 17 occupation say they weren't planning for an occupation that would go on week after week. It just hadn't occurred to them. And no one can say where things will go from here. Harsh weather could drive people away. Other hazards could undercut the movement. Police violence could frighten away would-be protesters, or it could galvanize the movement, as did the pepper spraying of unarmed women in Manhattan and police violence against occupiers in Oakland.

Another threat to the movement is violence on the part of the occupiers themselves, which would be used to justify police action and likely turn press coverage against the occupations. With increasing tensions and exhausted protesters, the nonviolent discipline of this movement will be severely tested.

Violence could also come from provocateurs seeking to discredit the Occupy movement. Within a month of the movement's launch there was a case of an admitted provocateur, an assistant editor at the right-wing magazine *American Spectator*, who tried, without success, to get Occupy and anti-war protesters to join him in pushing past security guards at the Smithsonian Museum of Air and Space in Washington, DC. Fortunately, the crowd refused to follow. Security guards responded by pepper spraying protesters, and the museum was closed for some hours. Most news reports attributed the scuffle to Occupy Wall Street protesters.

But the movement has important strengths that add to its resilience. It is radically decentralized, so a disaster at any one occupation will not bring down the others; in fact, the others can take action in support. There is no single leader who could be co-opted or assassinated. Instead, leadership is broadly shared, and leadership skills are being taught and learned constantly.

What's more, the autonomous groups within the movement that plan and carry out direct actions of all sorts are extremely difficult to contain. By choosing the targets of their actions wisely, they can further draw attention to institutions whose behavior calls into question their right to exist. When the legitimacy of large institutions crumbles, it is often just a matter of time before the support of government, stockholders, customers, and employees goes away, too. There is no institution that is "too big to fail." This is one way that nonviolent revolution happens.

New support is flowing in, some from unexpected sources. A group of Marine veterans has formed OccupyMARINES, which will work to recruit police and members of other branches of the military to support the occupations, and to nonviolently protect protesters from police assaults. The Marines also plan to help the occupations sustain themselves through cold weather. The group was inspired by a viral video showing Marine Sergeant Shamar Thomas dressing down the police for brutalizing protesters. "There is no honor in this," he shouted at the police. The wounding of Marine veteran Scott Olsen, who at twenty-four years old had already served two tours in Iraq, has further fired up fellow Marines. Olsen was critically injured by a police-fired projectile in an Oakland police action against occupiers.

Police, though often shown cracking down on occupations, have also expressed sympathy with the movement. In Albany, New York, state and city police declined to follow orders from the mayor to arrest and remove peaceful protesters. "We don't have those resources, and these people were not causing trouble," an official with the state patrol told the *Times Union* newspaper.

Will there come a time when there is no one willing to enforce orders to evict members of the 99% from occupation encampments—or from their homes, for that matter? And if popular support grows, will elected officials look to ally themselves with the movement, rather than suppress it? The fact that these are even questions shows how radically things have changed since a few hundred people occupied Zuccotti Park on September 17, 2011.

Whatever happens next, Occupy Wall Street has already accomplished something that changes everything. It has fundamentally altered the national conversation.

"A group of people started camping out in Zuccotti Park, and all of a sudden the conversation started being about the right things," says *The New York Times* columnist Paul Krugman. "It's kind of a miracle."

Now that millions recognize the injustice resulting from the power of Wall Street and giant corporations, that issue will not go away. The central question now is this: Will we build a society to benefit everyone? Or just the 1%?

The world becomes a very different place when members of the 99% stand up. The revolts in Egypt, elsewhere in the Middle East, and in Europe belie the story that popular uprisings are futile. The people occupying Zuccotti Park in lower Manhattan and in cities across the country have showed that Americans, too, can take a stand.

People who've experienced the power of having a voice will not easily go back to silence. People who've found self-respect will work hard to avoid a return to isolation and powerlessness; the Occupy Wall Street movement gives us reason to believe that *we the people* can take charge of our destinies. The 99% are no longer sitting on the sidelines of history—we are making history.

Sarah van Gelder is co-founder and executive editor of YES! Magazine *and YesMagazine.org.*

10 WAYS THE OCCUPY MOVEMENT CHANGES EVERYTHING

Many question whether this movement can really make a difference. The truth is that it is already changing everything. Here's how.

1. **It names the source of the crisis.**
   The problems of the 99% are caused by Wall Street greed, corrupt banks, and a corporate take-over of the political system.

2. **It provides a clear vision of the world we want.**
   We can create a world that works for everyone, not just the wealthiest 1%.

3. **It sets a new standard for public debate.**
   Those advocating policies and proposals must now demonstrate that their ideas will benefit the 99%. Serving only the 1% is no longer sufficient.

4. **It presents a new narrative.**
   The solution is no longer to starve government, but to free society and government from corporate dominance.

5. **It creates a big tent.**
   We, the 99%, are made up of people of all ages, races, occupations, and political beliefs, and we are learning to work together with respect.

6. **It offers everyone a chance to create change.**
   No one is in charge. Anyone can get involved and make things happen.

7. **It is a movement, not a list of demands.**
   The call for transformative structural change, not temporary fixes and single-issue reforms, is the movement's sustaining power.

8. **It combines the local and the global.**
   People are setting their own local agendas, tactics, and aims. But we also share solidarity, communication, and vision at the global level.

9. **It offers an ethic and practice of deep democracy and community.**
   Patient decision-making translates into wisdom and common commitment when every voice is heard. Occupy sites are communities where anyone can discuss grievances, hopes, and dreams in an atmosphere of mutual support.

10. **We have reclaimed our power.**
    Instead of looking to politicians and leaders to bring about change, we can see now that the power rests with us. Instead of being victims to the forces upending our lives, we are claiming our sovereign right to remake the world.

Developed by the staff of YES! Magazine and Steve Piersanti of Berrett-Koehler Publishers.

Photo by Brett Casper

NEW YORK CITY, October 1, 2011

PART I

OCCUPY WALL STREET

Who would have thought that a scrappy group of activists camped in a park with drums, tarps, cardboard, Sharpies, and some donated pizza could change the world?

How *did* that happen?

Andy Kroll's piece, on page 16, looks back to the critical early moments in which a traditional progressive rally was hijacked, top-down organizing gave way to "horizontal" activism, and hundreds settled in Zuccotti Park and declared an occupation.

You could argue that protesters made things more difficult for themselves by relying on consensus decision-making. David Graeber, who was there, thinks the move was audacious and brilliant—see page 22.

What was it like in Zuccotti Park on the night when occupiers and supporters awaited a threatened eviction? Marina Sitrin, one of the organizers, writes about this and other turning points— see page 27.

How inclusive is this movement? Can it claim to represent the diversity of the 99%? Hena Ashraf, a Muslim filmmaker of South Asian heritage, experienced first dismay at the racial blindness she encountered and then elation when her views were heard and incorporated. (See page 33.)

What about nonviolence? Nathan Schneider on page 39 explores the power of diverse, autonomous groups making decisions for themselves and rejecting violence without having anyone tell them to do so.

Naomi Klein, in her speech in Zuccotti Park (see page 45) says the Occupy Wall Street movement, along with sister movements around the world, are our best hope of dealing with huge global challenges like climate change, overfishing, and massive inequality.

CHAPTER 1

HOW OCCUPY WALL STREET REALLY GOT STARTED

ANDY KROLL

Months before the first occupiers descended on Zuccotti Park in lower Manhattan, before the news trucks arrived and the unions endorsed, before Michael Bloomberg and Michael Moore and Kanye West made appearances, a group of artists, activists, writers, students, and organizers gathered on the fourth floor of 16 Beaver Street, an artists' space near Wall Street, to talk about changing the world. There were New Yorkers in the room, but also Egyptians, Spaniards, Japanese, and Greeks. Some had played a part in the Arab Spring uprising; others had been involved in the protests catching fire across Europe. But no one at 16 Beaver knew they were about to light the fuse on a protest movement that would sweep the United States and fuel similar uprisings around the world.

The group often credited with sparking Occupy Wall Street is *Adbusters*, the Canadian anti-capitalist magazine that, in July, issued a call to flood lower Manhattan with ninety-thousand protesters. "Are you ready for a Tahrir moment?" the magazine asked. But that's not how Occupy Wall Street sprang to life. Without that worldly group that met at 16 Beaver and later created the New York City General Assembly, there might not have been an Occupy Wall Street as we know it today.

The group included local organizers, including some from New Yorkers Against Budget Cuts, but also people who'd taken part in uprisings all over the world. That international spirit would galvanize Occupy Wall Street, connecting it with the protests in Cairo's Tahrir Square and Madrid's Puerta del Sol, the heart of Spain's populist uprising. Just as a comic book about Martin Luther King Jr. and civil disobedience, translated into

Arabic, taught Egyptians about the power of peaceful resistance, the lessons of Egypt, Greece, and Spain fused together in downtown Manhattan. "When you have all these people talking about what they did, it opens a world of possibility we might not have been able to imagine before," says Marina Sitrin, a writer and activist who helped organize Occupy Wall Street.

Around thirty people showed up for those first gatherings at 16 Beaver earlier this summer, recall several people who attended. Some of them had just come from "Bloombergville," a weeks-long encampment outside New York City Hall to protest deep budget cuts to education and other public services, and now they itched for another occupation. As the group talked politics and the battered economic landscape in the United States and abroad, a question hung in the air: "What comes next?"

Begonia S.C. and Luis M.C., a Spanish couple who attended those 16 Beaver discussions, had an idea. (They asked that their full names not be used to avoid looking like publicity seekers.) In the spring, they had returned to Spain for the protests sweeping the country in reaction to staggering unemployment, a stagnant economy, and hapless politicians. On May 15, twenty-thousand *indignados*, "the outraged," had poured into Madrid's Puerta del Sol, transforming the grand plaza into their own version of Tahrir Square. Despite police bans against demonstrations, the plaza soon became the focal point of Spain's social media-fueled 15-M movement (named for May 15), which spread to hundreds of cities in Spain and Italy. When they returned to the United States, Begonia and Luis brought the lessons of 15-M with them. At 16 Beaver, they suggested replicating a core part of the movement in the United States: the general assembly.

In America, we march, we chant, we protest, we picket, we sit in. But the notion of a people's general assembly is a bit foreign. Put simply, it's a leader-less group of people who get together to discuss pressing issues and make decisions by pure consensus. The term "horizontal" gets tossed around to describe general assemblies, which simply means there's no hierarchy: Everyone stands on equal footing. Occupy Wall Street's daily assemblies shape how the occupation is run, tackling issues such as cleaning the park, public safety, and keeping the kitchen running. Smaller working groups handle media relations, outreach, sanitation, and more. In Spain, general assemblies are hugely popular, forming not just in the cities but in individual neighborhoods, bringing a few hundred people together each week. In some cases, Spanish assemblies have been formed to stop home evictions or immigrant raids.

Why not bring the general assembly to Manhattan, Begonia and Luis suggested. Some said general assemblies were too time-consuming and tedious, but in the end, the idea took hold.

On August 2, the deadline for President Obama and congressional Republicans to cut a debt ceiling deal before the country tipped into default, a small group—some from 16 Beaver, others not—held a general assembly next to the iconic bronze bull in Bowling Green Park, blocks south of Wall Street. Except what was meant to be an assembly became just another rally with speakers and microphones exhorting a mostly passive crowd.

Georgia Sagri, a Greek artist based in New York who was in the crowd that day, watched with dismay. She had also supported forming an assembly, having watched them take shape back in her native Greece. Sagri was tired of the same old rally with a single focus—the death penalty, jobless benefits, immigration reform, you name it. The general assembly, on the other hand, promised a discussion without fixating on an issue or a person. In an assembly, labels or affiliations didn't matter. There in Bowling Green Park, Sagri couldn't wait any longer, and so she and a few others "hijacked," in her words, the August 2 gathering, wrestling it away from your average protest and back in the direction of a real general assembly.

It took some time for the group to get the hang of it—Sitrin describes the early assemblies as "quite awkward"—but when they did, the New York City General Assembly, the Big Apple's own experiment in direct democracy, was born. When the assembly hit a snag, members would refer to a document titled "How to cook a pacific #revolution," a how-to guide for general assemblies written by the Spanish and translated into more than a half-dozen languages. The NYCGA met on Saturdays in Tompkins Square Park in the East Village at 5:30 p.m. and lasted as long as five and a half hours. Afterward, people would regroup at Odessa, Sitrin recalls, a popular diner among the activist set where, over pierogies and potato pancakes, the talk of politics and economics carried on deep into the night.

By that time, *Adbusters'* rallying cry was in the air. Ricocheting around the Web was the magazine's Occupy Wall Street poster, depicting a ballerina pirouetting atop Wall Street's charging bull, while behind her riot police emerged from the mist. *Adbusters* picked September 17 as its day of action. The New York City General Assembly had talked with members of *Adbusters* and made the decision to set its sights on the seventeenth as well. Buzz was forming around that date, and the NYCGA wanted to make a splash.

In other words, if *Adbusters* provided the inspiration, the NYCGA and other community groups provided the ground game that made Occupy Wall Street a reality. As the appointed day inched closer, the NYCGA settled on an ideal location for Occupy Wall Street: one Chase Manhattan Plaza, the former site of JPMorgan Chase's headquarters, just north of Wall Street. Then, on the eve of the big day, the New York Police Department fenced off the plaza. Organizers went back to their list of eight potential locations in Manhattan, ultimately settling on Zuccotti Park. Zuccotti wasn't ideal, but it was close to Wall Street.

No one in the NYCGA anticipated a monthlong protest emerging out of the events of September 17. It just happened. The occupiers really occupied. A small patch of land in the shadow of Ground Zero's Freedom Tower was transformed into a living, breathing community. The heavy-handed tactics of the NYPD helped, attracting coverage from the TV networks and landing Occupy Wall Street on the front pages of *The New York Times* and the *New York Post*. The outpouring surprised even the most seasoned activists. "The conversations we were having were about what happened on September 17," Sitrin says. "We never talked about what might happen three weeks after that."

As the protest wore on, the NYCGA became Occupy Wall Street's daily "people's assembly," meeting each night at 7 p.m. What's more, the idea for an assembly, which grew out of those 16 Beaver discussions, spread to Occupy protests from Boston to Los Angeles. In the eyes of Georgia Sagri, Luis M.C., and Begonia S.C., the widespread use of assemblies here in the United States connects these uprisings with those in Europe and the Middle East like never before. "The real strength of the general assembly comes from the Arab Spring, from Tahrir Square, from Greece and from Spain," Luis says.

Begonia adds: "The people are not here for the American economic crisis. They're here for the crisis of the world."

Just as in those early discussions this summer, the world has come to Occupy Wall Street. In Washington Square Park two Saturdays ago, a band of Egyptians marched through the lively crowd, the Egyptian flag dancing in the breeze. The Egyptians' signs supported Occupy Wall Street and demanded voting rights for Egyptians living abroad. Mayssa Sultan, an Egyptian American who was among the group, says her compatriots decided to support the occupation after hearing that Occupy Wall Street had taken inspiration from the Tahrir Square revolution. "The voices being heard at Occupy Wall Street and all the other occupied cities around the country are very similar to Tahrir," she says, "in that people who don't have work, don't have health care, are seeing education being pulled back—they are trying to make their voices heard."

On October 15, 2011, Occupy Wall Street truly went global.

In 951 cities in eighty-two countries around the world, people marching under the banner of "October 15" and "#Global-Change" protested income inequality, corrupt politicians, and economies rigged to benefit a wealthy few at the expense of everyone else.

The #GlobalChange protests were mostly peaceful, though they gave way to rioting in Rome. The same issues fueling #GlobalChange animated the thousands allied with Occupy Wall Street who, on the same day, poured into Times Square, Washington Square Park, and the streets of Manhattan, not to mention the hundreds more Occupy spin-off protests from Berkeley to Boston. It truly was a global day of action, one lifted by the momentum of those never-say-die occupiers hunkered down in Zuccotti Park, who, if not for that early group of activists thinking about the world and how to change it, might not be where they are today.

Andy Kroll is a reporter for Mother Jones. *His work has appeared in* The Wall Street Journal, *SportsIllustrated.com,* The Detroit News, Salon, *and TomDispatch.com, where he's an associate editor. This chapter first appeared in* Mother Jones *on October 17, 2011.*

CHAPTER 2

ENACTING THE IMPOSSIBLE:
MAKING DECISIONS BY CONSENSUS

DAVID GRAEBER

On August 2, at the very first meeting of what was to become Occupy Wall Street, about a dozen people sat in a circle in Bowling Green. The self-appointed "process committee" for a social movement we merely hoped would someday exist contemplated a momentous decision. Our dream was to create a New York General Assembly: the model for democratic assemblies we hoped to see spring up across America. But how would those assemblies actually operate?

The anarchists in the circle made what seemed, at the time, an insanely ambitious proposal. Why not let them operate exactly like this committee: by consensus.

It was, in the least, a wild gamble, because as far as any of us knew, no one had ever managed to pull off something like this before. Consensus process had been successfully used in spokescouncils—groups of activists organized into separate affinity groups, each represented by a single "spoke"—but never in mass assemblies like the one anticipated in New York City. Even the general assemblies in Greece and Spain had not attempted it. But consensus was the approach that most accorded with our principles. So we took the leap.

Three months later, hundreds of assemblies, big and small, now operate by consensus across America. Decisions are made democratically, without voting, by general assent. According to conventional wisdom this shouldn't be possible, but it is happening—in much the same way that other inexplicable phenomena like love, revolution, or life itself (from the perspective of, say, particle physics) happen.

The direct democratic process adopted by Occupy Wall Street

has deep roots in American radical history. It was widely employed in the civil rights movement and by the Students for a Democratic Society. But its current form has developed from within movements like feminism and even spiritual traditions (both Quaker and Native American) as much as from within anarchism itself. The reason direct, consensus-based democracy has been so firmly embraced by and identified with anarchism is because it embodies what is perhaps anarchism's most fundamental principle: that in the same way human beings treated like children will tend to act like children, the way to encourage human beings to act like mature and responsible adults is to treat them as if they already are.

Consensus is not a unanimous voting system; a "block" is not a "no" vote, but a veto. Think of it as the intervention of a high court that declares a proposal to be in violation of fundamental ethical principles—except in this case the judge's robes belong to anyone with the courage to throw them on. That participants know they can instantly stop a deliberation dead in its tracks if they feel it a matter of principle, not only means they do it rarely, it also means that a compromise on minor points becomes easier; the process toward creative synthesis is really the essence of the thing. In the end, it matters less how a final decision is reached—by a call for blocks or a majority show of hands—provided everyone was able to play a part in helping to shape and reshape it.

We may never be able to prove through logic that direct democracy, freedom, and a society based on principles of human solidarity are possible. We can only demonstrate it through action. In parks and squares across America, people have begun to witness it as they have started to participate. Americans grow up being taught that freedom and democracy are our ultimate values, and that our love of freedom and democracy is what defines us as a people—even as, in subtle but constant ways, we're taught that genuine freedom and democracy can never truly exist.

The moment we realize the fallacy of this teaching, we begin to ask: How many other "impossible" things might we pull off? And it is there, it is here, that we begin enacting the impossible.

David Graeber is an anarchist, anthropologist, writer, activist, and a Reader in Social Anthropology at Goldsmiths, University of London. This chapter first appeared in The Occupied Wall Street Journal *on October 23, 2011.*

CHAPTER 3

PRINCIPLES OF SOLIDARITY

THE OCCUPY WALL STREET GENERAL ASSEMBLY

What follows is a living document that will be revised through the democratic process of general assembly.

On September 17, 2011, people from all across the United States of America and the world came to protest the blatant injustices of our times perpetuated by the economic and political elites. On the seventeenth, we as individuals rose up against political disenfranchisement and social and economic injustice. We spoke out, resisted, and successfully occupied Wall Street. Today, we proudly remain in Liberty Plaza (also known as Zuccotti Park) constituting ourselves as autonomous political beings engaged in nonviolent civil disobedience and building solidarity based on mutual respect, acceptance, and love. It is from these reclaimed grounds that we say to all Americans and to the world, "Enough!" How many crises does it take? We are the 99% and we have moved to reclaim our mortgaged future.

Through a direct democratic process, we have come together as individuals and crafted these principles of solidarity, which are points of unity that include but are not limited to:

- engaging in direct and transparent participatory democracy;

- exercising personal and collective responsibility;

- recognizing individuals' inherent privilege and the influence it has on all interactions;

- empowering one another against all forms of oppression;

- redefining how labor is valued;

- the sanctity of individual privacy;

- the belief that education is a human right; and

- endeavoring to practice and support wide application of open source.

We are daring to imagine a new socio-political and economic alternative that offers greater possibility of equality. We are consolidating the other proposed principles of solidarity, after which demands will follow.

This is an official document crafted by the Working Group on Principles of Consolidation. The New York City General Assembly came to consensus on September 23, 2011 to accept this working draft and post it online for public consumption.

CHAPTER 4

THE CHILLS OF POPULAR POWER: THE FIRST MONTH OF OCCUPY WALL STREET

MARINA SITRIN

The reflections below are a small snapshot of what I have been feeling and thinking over these past six weeks. They were all written in the heat of the moment, without sleep and full of passion. I have only now begun to slow down a little and reflect more deeply with others on what has been launched, what we are creating, and what it could mean for social and political transformation.

Not that we did not intend it—we did of course—but a movement has begun that is vaster and deeper than most of us anticipated in such a short time. I do not pretend to understand yet why all of this exploded now, and even more, why people around the United States and the world have chosen to come together in directly democratic and horizontal forms. I am thrilled— inspired—but still sometimes taken by surprise.

September 21, 2011
Another amazing day in Liberty Plaza.

Today is day five of the occupation. Many people did not think it would last this long (myself included). Well, I should restate that—many people, often with lots of political experience in New York, thought it would not last. New people, people whose imaginations are totally free, people who are angry and simultaneously dreaming of a new world and who cannot imagine restrictions to that new world, believed that absolutely we would occupy the plaza, and they continue to not only believe it, but feel it will get bigger and broader. What is this based on? I am not sure. But so far, they are right.

Today, day five, the group in the plaza, which really is a

core group of a few hundred and many, many hundred more who flow in and out, is much more diverse than the first few days. There are people from more diverse backgrounds racially, more diverse age groups, including not just a few children here with their parents, and a number of working people from the area. In particular, some of the security guards from the 9/11 memorial, a block away, have been coming by for lunch and chatting with people, as have some construction workers. One of the 9/11 security guards I met is from Spain and he hopes the group continues and expands, as is happening in Spain.

As far as what a day looks like, there are workshops, information sharing, trainings, a mid-day and evening general assembly, and at least two marches. Today the marches were rallies for Troy Davis. After a spirited march this evening, the group came back into the plaza for the general assembly and then got word that there was a stay of execution for Troy Davis. People were exuberant. There was another march, and when the general assembly finally began, it began with a song. A young woman from Boston, who has been camping in the plaza since Saturday, taught many other young people the words—stanza by stanza— to "We Shall Overcome." There were many white beards also in the crowd who were singing in loud passionate voices. Reflecting again the crowd getting more—not less—diverse. When it came to "We Shall All Be Free," I got teary. It was the song, it was the stay of execution, and it was the community being built.

More soon. With inspiration and freedom,

Marina

We were heartbroken and enraged to hear later that night that the state had lifted the stay of execution, killing yet another black man.

Between this first e-mail dispatch that I wrote and the second, the level of organization in the plaza became much more sophisticated, with the few working groups that existed at the time of the occupation multiplying into dozens, from medical, legal, and food, to sanitation, safer spaces, and an elaborate library, to education, press, mediation, and conflict resolution. (NYCGA.net has the most updated list of working groups—over thirty-five at the time of writing this.) The group has also diversified on many levels, as the below dispatch begins to reflect.

September 30, 2011

As some of you know, when I am so moved, moved beyond words, I begin things with "imagine…"

So, imagine a few thousand people…no…more than a few…six thousand or seven thousand people. So many people that a large plaza near Wall Street cannot fit them, so they have to overflow onto the corners and sidewalks of the entire perimeter, and corners and sidewalks across the street on every side. Imagine that all of these people are there because they are fed up and angry with something related to the economic crisis and Wall Street.

Why are they there now? Why on this Friday afternoon at 3 p.m.? Maybe some are there because they heard on the Occupy Wall Street Web site that Radiohead was doing a concert. Maybe. Or maybe they came because they are members of the Transportation Workers Union, a union of thirty-eight thousand that voted unanimously the night before to support the occupation of Wall Street. Maybe. Or maybe they were from the Professional Staff Congress, the union of teachers, adjuncts, and graduate students from the City University system who also voted the night before to support the occupation. Maybe. Or, maybe it was people from the Malcolm X Grassroots Movement, who were part of organizing the later demonstration against police brutality—a demonstration that left from the plaza five thousand strong. Maybe. Or maybe they heard from a friend, neighbor, or the media that something has been happening near Wall Street. And maybe, it was all of these people. And more. Imagine your neighbor was there. She might have been.

Tonight was the largest and by far most diverse crowd the plaza has ever seen. There were pregnant women, babies, and children, along with grannies and white beards, and everyone in the middle. There were at least four wheelchairs, and all sorts of differently abled people. There were people from all over the world and a variety of races and backgrounds. No question the unions and students were there.

Can you now imagine this group having a democratic discussion? Imagine the people's mic, where people speak in short phrases and the group repeats them so all can hear. In the first week, up until tonight, the people's mic worked for a few hundred people—not ideally, but one can hear. With thousands, the people's mic has to be repeated not one time, not two times, but three. Each wave of sound representing another mass of people hearing the voice of the person speaking. Each wave of sound representing people actively listening by repeating. The facilitators (a team at this point) help remind the person speaking, by gently touching their arm, that they have to wait for each wave to finish before the next phrase is spoken.

Imagine the quiet of people listening, and the sound of the repetition of the words of the person speaking. Imagine the power of direct democracy moving through your body, along with thousands around you. I have chills writing this. I was moved beyond words this evening.

At this point, we—whoever we are—are too big for the plaza. We need to take over more parks, squares, and plazas and facilitate more horizontal discussions about what we want and desire. About the crisis and our alternatives. For me, our demand should be: Let us meet. Leave us alone so we can gather in our plazas, parks, and squares, in our union halls, schools, universities, churches, synagogues, and mosques, and leave us alone so we can find horizontal, democratic ways to discuss the crisis of our times and the many alternatives. Together.

With the chills of real democracy,
Marina

The piece below was written the day police had been autho-
rized by Mayor Bloomberg to support Brookfield Properties, the
semi-legal owners of the park, in a "temporary" eviction of the
park so as to "clean" it.

October 14, 2011

Tears again. The most beautiful sort of tears. Tears of inspiration—created by popular power.

The tears began at 6 a.m. at Liberty Plaza, or, better said,
with the thousands in and around Liberty Plaza. The outpouring
of solidarity quite literally filled the plaza to beyond overflowing.
I am exhausted and overwhelmed with emotion.

I did not know that popular power could bring with it such
an overwhelming sensation. It is a chill…a tremble that is both
incredibly powerful—feeling one's power with others—and also
a little scary, feeling how much power we can actually have
together, side by side.

As I slowly weaved my way through the masses of people,
many who began arriving at midnight, I walked with my tears
and my chills. I was weaving through groups of very young people, easily in their teens and early twenties, many people with
piercings, and others clearly going to work soon, some even in
suit jackets. There were older people, grandparents, and so many
of us in between. All differently dressed and of many different
races and ethnicities. Some groups came together, but most it
seemed came as individuals, or with a friend or two. There were
many union members there, I could tell by their shirts and hats,
though they did not seem to have been "mobilized" but rather were coming on their own, as many rank-and-file workers
have been doing every day.

I saw lots of old friends and *compañeros*…sort of like a
reunion, only we were all there to use our bodies to prevent

the eviction of our plaza. Our plaza. A place that has now been claimed by tens of thousands of New Yorkers and people from across the country. A plaza that is organized with direct democracy and assembly forms of decision making. A plaza that we have held and opened to people for three weeks today.

As I wandered on the outside of the plaza, the inside being impossible to enter, overflowing with people as it was, I would listen on and off to the general assembly. There were a few opportunities since the people's mic was now on four and even five waves. The number of waves (times phrases are repeated) indicates just how large the group is. Most nights we have two waves, which is around five hundred people. Three waves is more like a thousand. And four waves, at least fifteen hundred.

This morning, the waves of people repeated the invitation from the Direct Action Working Group to join them in linking arms and keeping the plaza. The response was resounding applause. There was no discussion, debate, or hesitation. Not only did people agree with shouts, whistles, and their fingers twinkling in the air, but with their bodies. As 7 a.m. approached, the time the mayor and Brookfield Properties said they would come into the plaza with the police and move people out, the people did not move.

There, with at least five thousand others, we waited to see what would happen. We were ready for whatever that might mean. But what was clear was that our bodies were talking. People stayed in the plaza. People stayed around the plaza. Our plaza.

And then, with the people's mic, five waves extending, just before 7 a.m., the announcement came. They backed down. We won! Popular power!

Marina Sitrin is the author of Horizontalism: Voices of Popular Power in Argentina *and the forthcoming,* Everyday Revolutions: Horizontalism and Autonomy in Argentina. *This chapter first appeared on MarinaSitrin.com between September 17 and October 14, 2011.*

CHAPTER 5

CLAIMING SPACE FOR DIVERSITY AT OCCUPY WALL STREET

HENA ASHRAF

When I arrived at Occupy Wall Street on September 29, a document called "The Declaration of the Occupation of New York City" was being introduced at the general assembly. The facilitator announced that this document would be disseminated to the media, to the Internet, and to everyone who planned to occupy other cities. This document, in other words, was extremely important.

The general assembly read it together, line by line. For me, the experience was powerful and moving. Then I turned and joined my friends, Thanu and Sonny, who were with two people I hadn't met before named Manissa and Natasha. They all had just returned from the first local meeting of South Asians for Justice.

Without meaning to do so, we had formed a South Asian bloc within the general assembly, which had grown a lot over the past few days and was noticeably more diverse. We began to discuss the document and our issues with it. We weren't the only ones with concerns; numerous people spoke up and requested changes. The facilitators wanted to go back to the agenda items, but I felt that if people wanted to discuss this document now, then that was what we should do.

Thanu, Sonny, Manissa, Natasha, and I felt that some language needed to be changed, beginning with the line that read: "As one people, formerly divided by the color of our skin, gender, sexual orientation, religion, or lack thereof, political party and cultural background, we acknowledge the reality: that there is only one race, the human race, and our survival requires the cooperation of its members."

Our first concern was that the phrase "formerly divided by"

was unrealistic and erased histories of oppression that marginalized communities have suffered. Our second was that the language about "the human race" felt out of touch.

We debated about whether to speak up. The facilitators requested that we e-mail any changes to them, or speak to them later. However, I felt our thoughts needed to be shared with the general assembly, not with just a few organizers over e-mail. Our impromptu bloc was urging me to speak up. So I did.

To take the floor, a person would shout, "Mic check!" and others would repeat this back until they had the attention of the whole general assembly. Then the speaker would speak their mind in phrases of a few words at a time, which were repeated by the entire crowd until the message was complete.

I started shouting, "Mic check!," got the crowd's attention, and said I felt the phrase erased histories of oppression. Unfortunately, even though four or five presumably white people had spoken up before me to suggest changes, a facilitator who was a man of color told me that this was a time for questions, not changes to the document. Talk about feeling shut down.

The main facilitator, a white man, said that the document and the paragraph was meant to reflect the future that we wanted, and that the phrase "formerly divided by" should stay. I again shouted, "Mic check!" and our spontaneous Brown Power crew again repeated my words after me. I reiterated that the phrasing erased much history and was idealistic and unrealistic. At this point I looked around and realized everyone was staring at me. It hit me what we were doing, that we were demanding a change.

The protestors at Occupy Wall Street had been saying that they would reach out to people of color in order to have them engage and help create real change, because, let's face it, the protests had been very white and people of color needed to be present and to speak up. I realized that we were helping to make that change happen.

The facilitators asked if our issue was an ethical concern and said that if it was, then it would have to be addressed. I said yes, thereby blocking the document from moving forward. Manissa thanked the crowd and facilitators for working with us, then explained that we wanted to replace the phrase "formerly divided by" with "despite" or "despite the divisions of."

The change was accepted by the general assembly. Our impromptu crew turned to each other to discuss what had happened, and people expressed their agreement with what we had done. However, we still felt that the paragraph as a whole needed to be changed. Sonny pointed out that the language still left invisible, or attempted to erase, the dynamics of power, something that was extremely inappropriate in a document claiming to address the so-called 99%.

After the general assembly was over, we approached the facilitators and explained our issues with the language. What came next was a long and difficult conversation. This was a very hard discussion to have. It hurt that we had to explain what is behind racism to a facilitator and to the people around him. It hurt that many tried to disrupt us. It hurt that it had to happen at all. At the same time, there were many people listening in and contributing constructively. We walked away realizing that we had spontaneously come together, demanded change, and created it in a movement we were in solidarity with. We also felt a need for constructive criticism.

Since that night, about a dozen of us, including myself, have become highly involved with Occupy Wall Street. We have joined working groups, conducted trainings, and facilitated meetings, all in order to make the space more inclusive. We started a blog (infrontandcenter.wordpress.com) that has brought critical discussion about the Occupy movement from around the country, and we have been claiming and changing the space at Occupy Wall Street itself.

Hena Ashraf is an independent filmmaker based in New York City. This chapter first appeared on HenaAshraf.com on September 30, 2011.

CHAPTER 6

DECLARATION OF THE OCCUPATION OF NEW YORK CITY

IN THEIR OWN WORDS, WHY PROTESTERS ARE OCCUPYING WALL STREET

As we gather together in solidarity to express a feeling of mass injustice, we must not lose sight of what brought us together. We write so that all people who feel wronged by the corporate forces of the world can know that we are your allies.

As one people, united, we acknowledge the reality: that the future of the human race requires the cooperation of its members; that our system must protect our rights, and upon corruption of that system, it is up to the individuals to protect their own rights, and those of their neighbors; that a democratic government derives its just power from the people, but corporations do not seek consent to extract wealth from the people and the Earth; and that no true democracy is attainable when the process is determined by economic power. We come to you at a time when corporations, which place profit over people, self-interest over justice, and oppression over equality, run our governments. We have peaceably assembled here, as is our right, to let these facts be known.

- They have taken our houses through an illegal foreclosure process, despite not having the original mortgage.

- They have taken bailouts from taxpayers with impunity, and continue to give executives exorbitant bonuses.

- They have perpetuated inequality and discrimination in the workplace based on age, the color of one's skin, sex, gender identity, and sexual orientation.

- They have poisoned the food supply through negligence and undermined the farming system through monopolization.
- They have profited off of the torture, confinement, and cruel treatment of countless animals and actively hide these practices.
- They have continuously sought to strip employees of the right to negotiate for better pay and safer working conditions.
- They have held students hostage with tens of thousands of dollars of debt on education, which is itself a human right.
- They have consistently outsourced labor and used that outsourcing as leverage to cut workers' health care and pay.
- They have influenced the courts to achieve the same rights as people, with none of the culpability or responsibility.
- They have spent millions of dollars on legal teams that look for ways to get them out of contracts in regards to health insurance.
- They have sold our privacy as a commodity.
- They have used the military and police force to prevent freedom of the press.
- They have deliberately declined to recall faulty products endangering lives in pursuit of profit.
- They determine economic policy, despite the catastrophic failures their policies have produced and continue to produce.
- They have donated large sums of money to politicians, who are responsible for regulating them.
- They continue to block alternate forms of energy to keep us dependent on oil.
- They continue to block generic forms of medicine that could save people's lives or provide relief in order to protect investments that have already turned a substantial profit.
- They have purposely covered up oil spills, accidents, faulty

bookkeeping, and inactive ingredients in pursuit of profit.

- They purposefully keep people misinformed and fearful through their control of the media.
- They have accepted private contracts to murder prisoners even when presented with serious doubts about their guilt.
- They have perpetuated colonialism at home and abroad.
- They have participated in the torture and murder of innocent civilians overseas.
- They continue to create weapons of mass destruction in order to receive government contracts.*

To the people of the world,

We, the New York City General Assembly occupying Wall Street in Liberty Square, urge you to assert your power.

Exercise your right to peaceably assemble, occupy public space, create a process to address the problems we face, and generate solutions accessible to everyone.

To all communities that take action and form groups in the spirit of direct democracy, we offer support, documentation, and all of the resources at our disposal.

Join us and make your voices heard!

*These grievances are not all-inclusive.

This document was accepted by the New York City General Assembly on September 29, 2011, with minor updates made on October 1, 2011. It is the first official, collective statement of the protesters in Zuccotti Park.

CHAPTER 7

NO LEADERS, NO VIOLENCE:
WHAT DIVERSITY OF TACTICS MEANS FOR OCCUPY WALL STREET

NATHAN SCHNEIDER

Those who extol nonviolent discipline might be disappointed to learn that Occupy Wall Street has officially embraced "diversity of tactics," a phrase that often serves as a byword for condoning acts of violence. However, the way that the Occupation movement has carried out this policy might lead us to think of this concept differently. For the occupiers, it is less a license for violence—which they have generally avoided—than a broader philosophy of coordinated, decentralized activism.

Since the early stages of the movement, those taking part have been in a deadlock on the question of nonviolence. At a planning meeting in Tompkins Square Park prior to September 17, I recall a young man in dark sunglasses saying, knowingly, "There is a danger of fetishizing nonviolence to the point that it becomes a dogma." In response, a woman added, quite astoundingly, that "nonviolence just means not initiating violence." The question of nonviolence was ultimately tabled that night and thereafter. "This discussion is a complete waste of time," someone concluded.

Property damage and self-defense, therefore, have remained on the table. The relevant points of the march guidelines later promulgated by Occupy Wall Street's Direct Action Committee are these:

- Don't instigate physical violence with cops or pedestrians.
- We respect diversity of tactics, but consider how our actions may affect the entire group.

This language, again, might seem like a way of saying that

individual protestors are free to use violence, especially in self-defense. But in practice the occupiers have kept nonviolent discipline quite well. Their self-defense against police violence has been mainly with cameras, not physical force (though when tensions escalate during confrontations with the police, one sometimes sees a few protesters coming very close to the precipice). There have been no cases of intentional property destruction that I know of.

One reason for this is surely common sense: When facing an essentially paramilitary institution like the NYPD, there's little hope that a few hundred or a few thousand protesters could stand much of a chance with violence. Another reason is the point made in the second guideline quoted above, which acknowledges that an act of violence would reflect on everyone in the movement, many of whose participants would not condone it.

So far, at least, what "diversity of tactics" has meant to the occupiers is not so much an openness to violence but a whole approach to direct action that comes out of anarchist thought. In this, "diversity of tactics" shares the heritage and logic of the open assemblies that are the heart of the occupation movement. Take this passage from a pamphlet on hand at occupied Liberty Plaza (also known as Zuccotti Park), *Anarchist Basics*:

> Affinity groups ["of 5 to 20 people"] decide on their own what they want to do and how they want to do it, and aren't obliged to take orders from any person on top. As such, they challenge top-down decision-making and organizing, and empower those involved to take direct action in the world around them...Affinity groups by nature are decentralized and non-hierarchical, two important principles of anarchist organizing and action.

Operating this way reflects the kind of values that many in the occupation movement insist on: individual autonomy, consensus decision-making, decentralization, and equality.

Consider, for instance, the two main events that brought public attention and sympathy to the movement: the arrest of nearly a hundred people on a march near Union Square on September 24 (which included an infamous pepper-spraying incident), and the approximately seven hundred arrested a week later on the Brooklyn Bridge. In both cases, the arrests directly followed instances of autonomous action by small groups, which splintered away from the plan established by the Direct Action Committee. (At Union Square, there was a dispute about whether to take the march back to Liberty Plaza or to the United Nations; at the Brooklyn Bridge, hundreds of marchers chose to spill onto the roadway rather than remaining on the narrow pedestrian walkway.) In both cases, too, the police responded to such autonomous action with violent overreaction, which in turn garnered tremendous interest from the media.

I have previously called for the movement to adopt more orderly kinds of civil disobedience actions, ones targeted specifically at the laws they oppose—on the model of lunch-counter sit-ins in the civil rights movement, for instance. However, I've been forced to recognize that the messy stuff seems to work.

My sense of the dynamics at play here is something like the following: The NYPD, as a hierarchical, highly structured organization, operates according to certain plans and procedures arranged in advance. Its commanders gain the best intelligence they can about what protesters intend to do and act accordingly. When the protesters act outside the plans police prepared for, or their plans aren't unified, the police feel they have no choice but to resort to a violent crackdown, which in turn highlights the protesters' own nonviolence in the media reports, and their movement grows. The net effect is that it almost seems as if the police are intentionally trying to help the movement, for that's what their every action seems to do.

We already know that power structures that rely on violence can be highly vulnerable to coordinated nonviolent action. During the civil rights movement, a structured and disciplined action in a segregated city, like a sit-in or Freedom Ride, had the capacity

to confront the system in a very direct way, presenting to the powerful a choice between violent overreaction and capitulation. Such
actions have since become ritualized and generally ineffective in
American protest movements.

Occupy Wall Street commends to us the anarchist insight
that, in much the same way, hierarchical command structures
are vulnerable to non-hierarchical action. If this is true, the real
strength of the 1999 Seattle mobilization against the World Trade
Organization—after which "diversity of tactics" entered activist
parlance—was not so much the particular tactics used, least of all
the window-breaking antics of "black blocs." It was the decentralized way in which such tactics were organized and deployed.

A major reason why traditional forms of civil disobedience
aren't well-suited to Occupy Wall Street is the fact that the occupiers aren't even capable of breaking the relevant laws in the first
place. While those in the civil rights movement could sit in the
wrong part of a segregated bus, the occupiers at Liberty Plaza
can't exactly flout campaign finance laws, or laws regarding the
regulation of banks. Such laws are simply beyond the reach of
most Americans—which is exactly the problem. Consequently,
the movement is being forced to resort not to civil disobedience
but to what political scientist Bernard Harcourt has proposed we
call "political disobedience":

> Civil disobedience accepted the legitimacy of political institutions,
> but resisted the moral authority of resulting laws. Political disobe-
> dience, by contrast, resists the very way in which we are governed:
> It resists the structure of partisan politics, the demand for policy
> reforms, the call for party identification, and the very ideologies that
> dominated the post-War period.

"Diversity of tactics" is a form of political disobedience *par
excellence*, since its emphasis on autonomy rather than authority
represents a direct contradiction to the kind of order that ordinary politics presupposes.

"Don't mistake the COMPLEXITY of this movement

for CHAOS," warns one of the many handmade cardboard signs at Liberty Plaza.

If it is true, as I've come to think, that a "diversity of tactics" has been meaningfully practiced by the Occupation movement even while remaining nonviolent, then traditional definitions of the phrase are in need of revision. Rather than merely granting permission to use violence, respecting a "diversity of tactics" is in its own right a robust approach to conducting resistance—and one that is arguably all the more powerful when it remains nonviolent. This was highlighted in the part of Naomi Klein's recent speech at Liberty Plaza that earned the loudest applause:

> Something else this movement is doing right: You have committed yourselves to nonviolence. You have refused to give the media the images of broken windows and street fights it craves so desperately. And that tremendous discipline has meant that, again and again, the story has been the disgraceful and unprovoked police brutality…Meanwhile, support for this movement grows and grows. More wisdom.

The data seem to support her. A widely cited Freedom House report from 2005 found that movements which rely on nonviolent methods are considerably more likely to result in democratic outcomes, rather than simply replacing one authoritarian system with another. This, especially, should carry weight for the Occupation movement, which strives so much to embody the ideals of a more democratic society in the means it uses to achieve one. If a permissive attitude toward violence is not a feature of the world one is working for, it should not be welcomed in one's movement.

Meanwhile, Erica Chenoweth and Kurt Schock have found through statistical studies that the effects of having a so-called "radical flank" in a resistance movement—having a violent minority—include a slightly lower success rate and a significantly lower level of public involvement. Canadian activists Philippe Duhamel and David Martin recognize this in their call for "a diversity of nonviolent tactics." They argue that "some tactics don't mix"; once violence enters the picture, it monopolizes the landscape of the conflict, co-opting other tactics and alienating potential participants. This certainly was the case on October 15, when a small number of people doing property destruction in Rome caused headlines like "Protests Turn Violent" to dominate the perception of an overwhelmingly nonviolent day of action in cities all over the world.

Only a month into the occupation, and less than three months since planning began in earnest, Occupy Wall Street is just beginning to have the robust affinity groups that a "diversity of tactics" approach requires. Some have led targeted actions like the disruption of a Sotheby's auction and a sit-in at a JPMorgan Chase bank branch. It is tactics like these—rather than mass arrests for obstructing traffic—that will begin to directly undermine the legitimacy of the powers the occupiers seek to target. And when causing such disruptions, remaining nonviolent will be crucial to ensuring that the disrupters keep their own legitimacy in the public eye.

The committee responsible for media relations for Occupy Wall Street has been preparing messaging—down to specific tweets—to use in case someone in the movement ends up using violence. Even those in the committee who aren't ultimately opposed to violence in principle recognize that such acts would be a serious challenge to the movement's credibility, both in the media and among those taking part in it. Given the commitment to a "diversity of tactics," though, just about anything can happen, and the committee often learns about it only after the fact.

Let's hope those tweets go unneeded.

Nathan Schneider writes about religion, reason, and violence for publications including The Nation, The New York Times, The Boston Globe, Commonweal, Religion Dispatches, AlterNet, *and* Truthout. *He is an editor for* Killing the Buddha *and for* Waging Nonviolence, *where this chapter first appeared on October 19, 2011.*

CHAPTER 8

THE MOST IMPORTANT THING IN THE WORLD

NAOMI KLEIN

I was honored to be invited to speak at Occupy Wall Street on Thursday night. Since amplification is (disgracefully) banned, and everything I say will have to be repeated by hundreds of people so others can hear (aka "the human microphone"), what I actually say at Liberty Plaza will have to be very short. With that in mind, here is the longer, uncut version of the speech.

I love you.

And I didn't just say that so that hundreds of you would shout "I love you" back, though that is obviously a bonus feature of the human microphone. Say unto others what you would have them say unto you, only way louder.

Yesterday, one of the speakers at the labor rally said, "We found each other." That sentiment captures the beauty of what is being created here. A wide-open space (as well as an idea so big it can't be contained by any space) for all the people who want a better world to find each other. We are so grateful.

If there is one thing I know, it is that the 1% loves a crisis. When people are panicked and desperate and no one seems to know what to do, that is the ideal time to push through their wish list of pro-corporate policies: privatizing education and social security, slashing public services, getting rid of the last constraints on corporate power. Amidst the economic crisis, this is happening the world over.

And there is only one thing that can block this tactic, and fortunately, it's a very big thing: the 99%. And that 99% is taking to the streets from Madison to Madrid to say, "No. We will not pay for your crisis."

That slogan began in Italy in 2008. It ricocheted to Greece

and France and Ireland and finally it has made its way to the square-mile where the crisis began.

"Why are they protesting?" ask the baffled pundits on TV. Meanwhile, the rest of the world asks: "What took you so long? We've been wondering when you were going to show up." And most of all: "Welcome."

Many people have drawn parallels between Occupy Wall Street and the so-called anti-globalization protests that came to world attention in Seattle in 1999. That was the last time a global, youth-led, decentralized movement took direct aim at corporate power. And I am proud to have been part of what we called "the movement of movements."

But there are important differences, too. For instance, we chose summits as our targets: the World Trade Organization, the International Monetary Fund, the G8. Summits are transient by their nature; They only last a week. That made us transient too. We'd appear, grab world headlines, then disappear. And in the frenzy of hyper-patriotism and militarism that followed the 9/11 attacks, it was easy to sweep us away completely, at least in North America.

Occupy Wall Street, on the other hand, has chosen a fixed target. And you have put no end date on your presence here. This is wise. Only when you stay put can you grow roots. This is crucial. It is a fact of the information age that too many movements spring up like beautiful flowers but quickly die off. It's because they don't have roots. And they don't have long-term plans for how they are going to sustain themselves. So when storms come, they get washed away.

Being horizontal and deeply democratic is wonderful. But these principles are compatible with the hard work of building structures and institutions that are sturdy enough to weather the storms ahead. I have great faith that this will happen.

Something else this movement is doing right: You have committed yourselves to nonviolence. You have refused to give the media the images of broken windows and street fights it craves so desperately. And that tremendous discipline has meant that, again and again, the story has been the disgraceful and unprovoked police brutality, which we saw more of just last night. Meanwhile, support for this movement grows and grows more wisdom.

But the biggest difference a decade makes is that in 1999, we were taking on capitalism at the peak of a frenzied economic boom. But to be honest with you, while the good times rolled, taking on an economic system based on greed was a tough sell, at least in rich countries.

Ten years later, it seems as if there aren't any more rich countries. Just a whole lot of rich people. People who got rich looting the public wealth and exhausting natural resources around the world.

The point is, today everyone can see that the system is deeply unjust and careening out of control. Unfettered greed has trashed the global economy. And it is trashing the natural world as well. We are overfishing our oceans, polluting our water with fracking and deepwater drilling, and turning to the dirtiest forms of energy on the planet, like the Alberta tar sands. And the atmosphere cannot absorb the amount of carbon we are putting into it, creating dangerous atmosphere warming. The new normal is serial disasters, economic and ecological.

These are the facts on the ground. They are so blatant, so obvious, that it is a lot easier to connect with the public than it was in 1999, and to build the movement quickly.

We all know, or at least sense, that the world is upside down: We act as if there is no end to what is actually finite—fossil fuels and the atmospheric space to absorb their emissions. And we act as if there are strict and immovable limits to what is actually bountiful—the financial resources to build the kind of society we need.

The task of our time is to turn this around: to challenge this false scarcity. To insist that we can afford to build a decent, inclusive society—while at the same time, respect the real limits to what the earth can take.

What climate change means is that we have to do this

on a deadline. This time our movement cannot get distracted, divided, burned out, or swept away by events. This time we have to succeed. And I'm not talking about regulating the banks and increasing taxes on the rich, though that's important.

I am talking about changing the underlying values that govern our society. That is hard to fit into a single media-friendly demand, and it's also hard to figure out how to do it. But it is no less urgent for being difficult.

That is what I see happening in this square. In the way you are feeding each other, keeping each other warm, sharing information freely, and providing health care, meditation classes, and empowerment training. My favorite sign here says, "I care about you." In a culture that trains people to avoid each other's gaze, to say, "Let them die," that sign carries a deeply radical statement.

A few final thoughts. In this great struggle, here are some things that don't matter:

- what we wear;
- whether we shake our fists or make peace signs;
- whether we can fit our dreams for a better world into a media sound bite.

And here are a few things that do matter:

- our courage;
- our moral compass;
- how we treat each other.

We have picked a fight with the most powerful economic and political forces on the planet. That's frightening. And as this movement grows from strength to strength, it will get more frightening. Always be aware that there will be a temptation to shift to smaller targets—like, say, the person sitting next to you at this meeting. After all, that is a battle that's easier to win.

Don't give in to the temptation. I'm not saying don't call each other on shit. But this time, let's treat each other as if we plan to work side by side in struggle for many, many years to come. Because the task before will demand nothing less.

Let's treat this beautiful movement as if it is the most important thing in the world. Because it is. It really is.

Naomi Klein is an award-winning journalist, syndicated columnist, and author of the bestselling book, The Shock Doctrine: The Rise of Disaster Capitalism. *This chapter is the transcript of a speech delivered at Occupy Wall Street on October 6, 2011, and originally published in* The Occupied Wall Street Journal *on October 8, 2011.*

Photo by Fran Korten

SEATTLE, October 15, 2011

PART II

WHAT NEEDS TO CHANGE

When 1% of the population controls the bulk of the wealth and power, the resulting inequality poisons our entire society. That's the point Richard Wilkinson makes in his interview with Brooke Jarvis on page 52.

But how do we restructure our economy so that it benefits the 99% instead of just the 1%?

A crucial step is to redesign the money and banking system to shift power from Wall Street to Main Street, says David Korten on page 55. He elaborates six key changes to feed resources to the Main Street economy, which meets actual human needs, instead of to the Wall Street economy, which feeds greed and speculation.

Another key is to shift taxes so that the wealthiest pay more. Progressive taxation allows us to invest in transportation, schools, and other public goods while preventing the cancerous growth of inequality. Chuck Collins on page 61 shows three immediate ways to make the tax system fairer.

We also need living-wage jobs that preserve and restore the soil, water, air, and other natural resources we rely on. We can do that by building locally rooted economies. Sarah van Gelder and Doug Pibel's article on (page 63) shows how to start.

These are just some of the ways to turn our unfair economy on its head and put the well-being of ordinary people, their communities, and the planet first.

CHAPTER 9

HOW INEQUALITY POISONS SOCIETY AND EQUITY BENEFITS EVERYONE:
AN INTERVIEW WITH RICHARD WILKINSON

BROOKE JARVIS

"We are the 99%." It's been perhaps the strongest rallying cry of the Occupy Wall Street movement—and for good reason. Millions are struggling for food, housing, and health care, while the incomes of the richest reach new heights.

But Occupy Wall Street has become a movement not only for the 99%, but also for people who recognize the failures of our current economic system despite having reaped huge benefits from it. "Our system needs fundamental change," writes one self-identified 1%-er in solidarity with Occupy Wall Street. "If it's not working for everyone, it's not working." She's right, in fact. British epidemiologist Richard Wilkinson has found that economic inequality has a host of corrosive impacts on whole societies, harming even those at the top of the pile. I sat down with Wilkinson to discuss the surprising importance of equality—and the best ways to build it.

Brooke: You've studied the impact of inequality on public health for a long time. Did any of your recent findings surprise you?

Richard: Oh, all of them. For many years, people working in public health have looked for a link between poverty and social problems like mental illness, crime, and infant mortality. We thought that once you found the relationship between income and death rates, for example, you would be able to predict what a state's death rate would be. Actually, though, that doesn't produce a good prediction. It turns out that what matters aren't the incomes themselves, but how unequal they are. If you're a more unequal state, the same level of income produces a higher death rate.

In less equal societies, we find perhaps eight times the number of teenage births per capita, ten times the homicide rate, three times the rate of mental illness. We know from the findings that it's the status divisions themselves that create the problems. It's almost impossible to find any other consistent explanation.

Brooke: How does thinking about these problems in terms of inequality rather than poverty change how we grapple with them?

Richard: I think people have been worried by the scale of social problems in our societies—feeling that though we're materially very successful, a lot of stuff is going wrong, and we don't know why. The media are always full of these social problems, and they blame parents or teachers or lack of religion or whatever. It makes an important difference to people to have an analysis that really fits, not only in a sort of academic way, but also that fits intuitions that people have had. People have intuited for hundreds of years that inequality was divisive and socially corrosive.

Inequality has psychosocial effects—the impact of living with anxiety about our feelings of superiority or inferiority. If you grow up in an unequal society, your actual experience of human relationships is different. Your idea of human nature changes. For instance, in more equal countries or more equal states, two-thirds of the population may feel they can trust others in general, whereas in the more unequal countries or states, it may drop as low as 15 percent or 25 percent.

Brooke: Once we become aware of the impact of inequality on all of these social ills, what do we do about it?

Richard: Countries seem to get their greater equality in quite different ways. Sweden, for example, uses the big government way: There are big differences in earnings, which are redistributed through taxes and benefits. It has a large welfare state. Japan, on the other hand, has smaller income differences to start with, does much less redistribution, and doesn't have such high social expenditure. But both countries do very well—they're among the more equal countries and their health and social outcomes are very good.

But we can't just rely just on taxes and benefits to increase equality—the next government can undo them all at a stroke. We've got to get this structure of equality much more deeply embedded in our society. I think that means more economic democracy, or workplace democracy, of every kind. We're talking about friendly societies, mutual societies, employee ownership, employee representatives on the board, cooperatives—ways in which business is subjected to democratic influence. The bonus culture is only possible because the people at the top are not answerable to the employees at all. Employee ownership turns a company into a community. The chief executive becomes answerable to employees. You might vote for your boss to have, I don't know, three times as much income as you—but not three hundred or four hundred times more.

Embedding greater equality and more democratic accountability in our institutions does much more than just changing income distribution or wealth distribution. And, a number of studies show that if you combine even partial employee ownership, you get quite reliable increases in productivity. This is about how we work better together.

Brooke Jarvis is YES! Magazine's *web editor and a regular contributor to* YES! *This chapter is adapted from an article that originally appeared on YesMagazine.org on March 4, 2010.*

CHAPTER 10

SIX WAYS TO LIBERATE MAIN STREET FROM WALL STREET

DAVID KORTEN

The Occupy Wall Street protests have achieved a remarkable breakthrough. They have penetrated the filter of the corporate media and captured the imagination of America and the world. They have focused attention on Wall Street banks and corporations as the primary threat to U.S. and global prosperity and security. And they have sparked a much needed conversation on the economy's values, purpose, and structure.

It is now up to all of us to build on the opening this movement has created to liberate Main Street from Wall Street.

Wall Street is the symbolic center of an economic system that works for the 1% at the expense of the 99%. It uses its outsized financial and media muscle to corrupt government and deepen the divide. Over the past thirty years, virtually all the benefit of U.S. economic growth has gone to the richest 1% of Americans. Effective tax rates for the very rich are at historic lows and many of the most profitable corporations pay no taxes at all.

Despite the crash of 2008, the financial assets of America's billionaires and the idle cash of the most profitable corporations are now at historic highs. Forbes magazine's list of the world's billionaires set two records in 2011: total number (1,210) and combined wealth ($4.5 trillion)—equal to the German GDP. The biggest challenge facing America's 1% is figuring out where to park all their cash.

Most of the individuals and corporations that hold the cash have lost interest in long-term investments that build and expand strong enterprises. Corporations are using their stores of cash primarily to buy back their own stock, invest in off-shoring American jobs, acquire control of other companies, and pay generous dividends to shareholders and exorbitant bonuses to management. The substantial majority of trades in financial markets are made by high-speed computers in securities held for fractions of a second to manipulate the market and profit from minor variations in stock prices. While business pundits refer to this trading as investment, it is not. Investment puts people to work in productive enterprises that build a strong economy.

Our banking industry and corporations did not always behave this way.

America is a tale of two economies. The Wall Street economy is accountable only to faceless financial markets and devoted to financial deception, manipulation, and speculation to maximize financial returns to its most powerful players. The Main Street economy is directly accountable to real people who have a natural interest in building healthy communities with thriving local economies and natural environments.

It Was Class Warfare, and Wall Street Won

After Wall Street drove the nation into the Great Depression of the 1930s, the Roosevelt administration enacted significant financial reforms. Those reforms put in place a system of money, banking, and investment based on community banks, mutual savings and loans, and credit unions. We had laws that prohibited one bank from owning another and severely limited the number of branches a bank could operate. These institutions provided loans to individuals and financial services to Main Street businesses that employed Americans to produce and trade real goods and services in response to community needs and opportunities. Corporate shares were held by individuals who knew the companies they owned.

The Main Street economy, which Wall Street interests now dismiss as quaint and antiquated, financed U.S. victory in World War II, the creation of a strong American middle class, an unprecedented period of economic stability and prosperity, and American world leadership in industry and technology. It also made the American dream of a secure and comfortable life in return for hard work and playing by the rules a reality for a substantial majority of Americans.

In the 1970s, Wall Street interests mobilized to use their financial and media power to re-establish control of the economy. It was class warfare, and Wall Street won.

Their primary targets were the regulations that limited the size and function of banks and other financial institutions. Step by step they transferred the power to create and allocate credit from locally owned, independent Main Street financial institutions—community banks, mutual savings and loans, and credit unions—to Wall Street institutions that had no particular interest in investments that create community wealth.

Wall Street institutions quickly developed a more profitable business model. The model has come to feature excessive fees and usurious interest rates for ordinary customers, financing speculation, luring the unwary into mortgages they cannot afford, bundling the resulting junk mortgages into derivatives sold as triple-A securities, betting against the sure-to-fail derivative products so created, extracting subsidies and bailouts from government, laundering money from drug and arms traders, and off-shoring profits to avoid taxes. Much of what provides profits to Wall Street either is, or should be, illegal.

Banking That Works for Everyone

The consequences of these activities are legion and have prompted hundreds of thousands of protesters to pour into the streets across the United States and the world. The effects include the erosion of the middle class, an extreme concentration of wealth and power, a costly financial collapse, persistent high unemployment, massive housing foreclosures, collapsing environmental systems, the hollowing out of U.S. industrial, technological, and research capacity, huge public and international trade deficits, and the corruption of our political institutions. Wall Street has profited at every step and declared its experiment with deregulation and tax cuts for the wealthy a great success. It argues that to fix the mess created by this experiment, we must grant more of the same.

Our economy depends on Wall Street institutions only because those institutions got the rules rewritten to give themselves control over much of the nation's money and productive resources. Every need we now depend on those institutions to fulfill can be better served by institutions with strong roots in Main Street.

Here are six steps we can take to liberate Main Street from Wall Street and build a democratically accountable economy based on sound market principles.

1.   Reverse the process of bank consolidation and rebuild a national system of community-based, community-accountable financial institutions devoted to building community wealth. Break up the mega-banks into independent, locally owned financial institutions backed by tax and regulatory policies that favor community financial institutions.

2.   Implement appropriate regulatory and fiscal measures to secure the integrity of financial markets and the money and banking system. Such measures properly favor productive investment, limit banking institutions to basic banking functions, and render financial speculation and other unproductive financial games illegal and unprofitable.

3.   Create a state partnership bank, modeled on the state Bank of North Dakota, in each of the fifty states to serve as a depository for state financial assets. Such banks can use their funds to spur community investment by partnering with community financial institutions within the state on loans to local home buyers and locally owned enterprises engaged in construction, agriculture, industry, and commerce.

4.   Restructure the Federal Reserve to limit its responsibility to managing the money supply, subject it to federal oversight and public accountability, and require that all newly created funds be applied to funding green public infrastructure. Assign what is currently the Fed's responsibility for the regulation of banks and so-called "shadow banking" institutions to specialized regulatory agencies with clear public accountability.

5.   Create a Federal Recovery and Reconstruction Bank (FRRB) to finance critical green infrastructure projects designated by Congress. Fund this bank with the money that the Federal Reserve creates when it determines a need to expand the money supply. Rather than introducing the new money into the economy through Wall Street banks, as is currently the Fed's practice, introduce the money through the FRRB to fund projects that directly and immediately serve the common good. This reform makes funding available for critical projects without drawing on tax revenues.

6.   Rewrite international trade and investment rules to encourage national ownership, self-reliance, and self-determination. Bring international rules into alignment with the foundational assumptions of trade theory that the ownership of productive assets belongs to citizens of the country in which those assets are located and that trade between nations is balanced. Hold corporations that operate in multiple countries accountable for compliance with the laws of each country of operation.

Given the government's failure to restructure the banking system, another financial crash is a near certainty. That will be a defining moment. We need to be prepared with a plan to transform the money and banking system from one that benefits only the 1% to one that benefits all.

We need not, however, wait for the next crash. Citizens of all walks of life can act immediately to advance public understanding of the issues raised here, move accounts from Wall Street to Main Street financial institutions, promote cooperative or nonprofit ownership of financial institutions, and advocate legislation to restructure the system.

None of the steps in this six-part agenda will be easy. The forces aligned to maintain the status quo are formidable. But Occupy Wall Street and the 99% movement have created a new conversation that could lead to change with a speed and on a scale that previously seemed unimaginable.

David Korten is co-founder and board chair of YES! *Magazine and co-chair of the New Economy Working Group. He is the author of* Agenda for a New Economy *and the international best seller,* When Corporations Rule the World. *This chapter is based on the report, "How to Liberate America from Wall Street Rule," which is available for free at neweconomyworkinggroup. org/report/how-liberate-america-wall-street-rule.*

CHAPTER 11

A FAIR TAX SYSTEM:
THREE PLACES TO START

CHUCK COLLINS

Over the last half-century, we've witnessed a dramatic shift in who pays taxes. The responsibility has moved off the very wealthy and onto the middle class, off the global corporations and onto small businesses, and off the federal government and onto state and local budgets.

According to a new report from Wealth for the Common Good, an organization that I co-founded, the wealthy have received massive tax cuts, not only under President George W. Bush but for decades before his election. The top 1% of taxpayers, those with incomes of $500,000 or more, have seen their share of income paid in federal taxes decline from 60 to 33.6 percent between 1960 and 2004. During President Bush's eight years in office, Congress expanded tax cuts to Americans with incomes over $250,000, adding another $700 billion to the national debt.

Meanwhile, the share of household income that middle-class households pay in federal taxes actually increased slightly, from 15.9 to 16.1 percent.

Congress has failed to close tax loopholes for global corporations, allowing thousands of profitable U.S. companies to pay no corporate income taxes—at all—between 1998 and 2008. For example, General Electric generated $10.3 billion in pre-tax income in 2009, but ended up paying nothing in U.S. taxes.

Global corporations dodge taxes by setting up subsidiaries in countries that have low or no corporate income tax. They claim their profits are made there, which allows them to avoid paying U.S. taxes, while asking the American people to pay for their losses. A small business has to compete against companies that unfairly utilize such loopholes.

When big corporations and high-income individuals don't pay their share, the bills get passed to the middle class and our debt grows. That's hard to appreciate until things start to hit home in the form of cuts to public schools, veterans' services, mass transit, and thousands of other services on which we depend every day. Our public service commons have been chronically underfunded for the last forty years.

Reversing the tax shift would not only reduce the tax burden borne by the bottom 70 percent of taxpayers; it would also allow us to make long-overdue investments in upgrading our aging public infrastructure and defending the commons.

In the United States, we tend to take for granted the advanced commons (public infrastructure, property, and knowledge institutions) that our ancestors built. We're like fish who swim in an ocean of publicly funded services without seeing the water around us. Taxes are the way we pay for this healthy common heritage, ensuring that they exist for the next generation.

Here are three things you can do to support the commons:

1.   Join your local occupation, or start a new one. Bring a sign showing how you feel about unfair taxation and talk with fellow protestors to find ways to bring this issue to light.

2.   Help close overseas tax havens. Business for Shared Prosperity and Wealth for the Common Good are enlisting investors and small businesses to speak out against tax haven abuse. Go to businessagainsttaxhavens.org to learn more.

3.   Support a financial speculation tax. A modest financial speculation tax on Wall Street transactions would raise over $150 billion annually in urgently needed revenue. See the campaigns page at wealthforcommongood.org for more information.

Chuck Collins is a senior scholar at the Institute for Policy Studies where he directs the Program on Inequality and the Common Good. This chapter first appeared on YesMagazine.org on April 12, 2010.

This book has some good points but is filled with liberal demagoguery. (i.e. lies)

CHAPTER 12

HOW TO CREATE LIVING-WAGE JOBS THAT ARE GOOD FOR THE PLANET

SARAH VAN GELDER AND DOUG PIBEL

Officially, the "Great Recession" ended in the second quarter of 2009. For some people, the recovery is well under way. Corporate profits are at or above pre-recession levels, and the CEOs of the 200 biggest corporations averaged over $10 million in compensation in 2010—a 23 percent increase over 2009.

But for most Americans, there's no recovery. Twenty-five million are unemployed, under-employed, or have given up looking for work. Forty-five percent of unemployed people have been without a job for more than twenty-seven weeks, the highest percentage since the Bureau of Labor Statistics started keeping track in 1948.

American workers have become expendable to many of the corporations that run the economy; NAFTA and other trade deals opened the floodgates to outsourcing. Other jobs are being eliminated, or hours, pay, and benefits are being cut.

As corporations amass greater power, wealth, and influence, they successfully lobby for tax breaks and federal subsidies and set the national policy agenda. And as long as they continue to cut jobs, the economy will not have sufficient demand to recover.

Real Solutions

Leaders in both parties tell us growth is what's needed, but the evidence suggests growth alone won't help. GDP has grown steadily, but since the official end of the recession, virtually all of the new income has gone to corporate profits, according to a May report by the Center for Labor Market Studies at Northeastern University. None of the increased GDP has gone to boost wages and salaries.

More importantly, since World War II, growth has been built on cheap energy. Now the easy-to-pump oil is nearly used up, and the cost of extraction is rising. At the same time, we've used up the earth's capacity to absorb climate-changing gases and other forms of pollution. Changes in the delicate balance of atmospheric gases are already disrupting the climate, and extreme weather events are happening with increasing frequency.

So how do we create an economy that provides dignified livelihoods to all who are willing to work, without undermining the natural systems we, and our children, rely on?

A real solution requires a vision that is both humble in terms of the material wealth we can expect and ambitious about the fairness, mutual support, and quality of life we can build.

That means building our local economies so they can sustain our families while also sustaining the natural world, which we rely on for our future.

1. Local Economies, Local Ecosystems

Strong local and regional economies are the way to build a sustainable and resilient recovery. Small businesses actually create more jobs and innovation than big corporations, and entrepreneurs with long-term stakes in their local environment and economy have both the means and the motivation to protect them. There are many simple ways individuals and communities can support the transition back to local economies.

- Buy local goods and services and keep money circulating in the Main Street economy, where new jobs are most likely to be created.

- Bank local, too. Credit unions, community-rooted banks, and state banks invest in the local economy, instead of siphoning off our bank deposits to use for global speculation.

- Start with strengths. Build economies from the grass-roots up, starting with existing assets, whether that's a vibrant local arts scene, farmland, or a hospital.

- Use wasted resources. Instead of demolishing and landfilling obsolete buildings, disassemble them and sell the components. Other common wastes: used clothes and books, unharvested fruit trees, and church kitchens that could be health department certified for food processing start-ups.

- Do it cooperatively. Home health care workers, house cleaners, grocery store clerks, and laundry workers have all become worker-owners of successful cooperatives.

- Allow communities to control their resources. Community-controlled forests are more likely to be sustainably managed; sustainable agriculture is more labor-intensive but less polluting. Sustainable and fair practices create jobs that last while boosting local resilience.

- Keep ownership human. When owners are workers, customers, or the community at large, an enterprise can operate in accordance with multiple values, such as human well-being, the good of future generations, and ecological health.

2. Redefining Middle-Class

To live within our means as we approach the end of the era of cheap energy and seemingly limitless growth, we'll need to produce and consume less stuff. That may mean less paid work available, at least in some sectors of the economy, so it makes sense to share those jobs and work fewer hours.

A shorter workweek could benefit those who are working too much while opening new jobs for the unemployed. Productivity increases when workers aren't overstretched. Profits now going to the wealthiest 1% could be distributed to workers so they could afford to work fewer hours and have more time for the rest of life.

Working less also means we have more time to do things for ourselves and for our neighbors. These informal exchanges among neighbors help reweave a community fabric that has been badly frayed by overstressed lives. Once you get the tools to repair your bicycle, you can fix other people's bikes or teach them how. When you're canning jam, it's easy to make some extra for gifts and exchanges.

With a strong community DIY ethic, people can live with less money, so they can afford to spend less time at a job and more on building the rich networks and practical skills that will enhance our resilience in an uncertain future.

3. Build People Power

We are still a wealthy country. We could use our tax dollars to put Americans to work replacing obsolete energy, water, transportation, and waste systems with green infrastructure that can serve us in the resource-constrained times ahead.

We could invest in universal health coverage, which offers people the security to risk launching new businesses and helps make shorter workweeks more feasible. We could fully fund education and job training.

We could save money by cutting the bloated military budget, oversized prison populations, and the drug war. And we'd have enough money if everyone—including the wealthiest Americans and large corporations—paid taxes at the rates they paid during the Clinton administration.

To get these sorts of changes, we need the American government to work for all of us, not just for corporations.

Powerful moneyed interests won't willingly give back the power that has allowed them to acquire most of America's wealth. We need strong people's movements to get government to work for ordinary Americans. That's the way American workers won the eight-hour day, women secured the right to vote, and African Americans ended segregation.

Enlightened politicians may cooperate with these movements, but they cannot lead them. We the people will have to set our own agenda and insist that government respond.

Sarah van Gelder and Doug Pibel wrote this article for "New Livelihoods," the Fall 2011 issue of YES! Magazine. *Sarah is executive editor and Doug is managing editor of* YES! Magazine.

Photo by Scott Eisen

BOSTON, October 5, 2011

PART III

WE HAVE THE POWER

Through the Occupy Wall Street movement we're redefining power, learning new ways to make change, and winning back our political self-respect. Instead of petitioning the powerful for change, we're making it happen ourselves. Instead of taking direction from leaders, each of us can claim the right as a sovereign individual to be part of powerful collective action.

But do marches and occupations really make a difference? And how do we take the next steps to build power for the 99%?

Thomas Linzey and Jeff Reifman on page 70 tell stories of communities around the United States—especially those resisting hydrofracking—that are using local lawmaking to end corporate "personhood" and determine their own futures.

Ralph Nader reminds us of past victories accomplished via organized, persistent street action, and through the willingness of people in all walks of life to "speak out and stand tall." See page 74.

Rebecca Solnit on page 77 ties the Occupy Wall Street movement to the revolutions of the Arab Spring and the uprisings in Europe, showing that ordinary people are often strengthened and transformed by such upheavals.

Sarah van Gelder wraps up this section with a list of 10 Ways to Support the Occupy Wall Street Movement on page 83. Whether or not you choose to sleep outside with your local occupiers, there are many, many ways to get involved.

CHAPTER 13

HOW TO PUT THE RIGHTS OF PEOPLE AND NATURE OVER CORPORATE RIGHTS

THOMAS LINZEY AND JEFF REIFMAN

The history of populist uprisings like Occupy Wall Street is far from reassuring. The last one to have any staying power was the populist farmers revolt of the 1800s, and it was aggressively dismantled by everyone from the two major political parties to the banks and railroad corporations of its day.

Most revolts are snuffed out well before their efforts affect the political scene—not because their ideas and issues aren't relevant, but because the major institutional players within the system-that-is attempt to snag the power and energy for their own. In the eyes of the Democratic Party or the national environmental groups, this revolt is merely an opportunity to assimilate newly emerging troops back into those groups' own ineffective organizing. Yet, if those institutional groups had actually been effective all of these years, why the need for a revolt at all?

It's when these revolts become mainstreamed by their "friends" within existing institutions that they lose their steam and become mere footnotes in an endless list of revolts that burned out early. The pundits and "experts" are already trying to put this revolt in its place. A recent *New York Times* editorial declared that it "isn't the job of these protesters to write legislation." That, the editorial argued, was what the national politicians need to do. The *Times* couldn't be more wrong.

If the Occupy movement is to succeed over time, it must follow the lead of community rights building efforts that have begun to dismantle the body of law that perpetually subordinates people, community, and nature to wealthy corporate minorities. For example:

- In November 2010, Pittsburgh's city council stripped corporations seeking to drill for natural gas of their corporate personhood rights, protections of the commerce and contracts clauses of the U.S. and Pennsylvania Constitutions, and the right to pre-empt community ordinances with federal or state law.
- In March 2011, for the first time since Ecuador added rights for nature to its Constitution, a judge stopped destructive corporate development in a suit brought by ordinary residents on behalf of the Vilcabamba River.
- This November, Spokane, Washington residents will vote on Proposition One which 1) grants neighborhoods complete control over local development, 2) affords rights and protections to the Spokane River and aquifer, 3) grants constitutional protections to employees in the workplace and 4) makes people's rights superior to corporate rights.

These communities, and many like them, have begun adopting Community Bills of Rights, which elevate the rights of people and nature above the rights of corporations. It's not another exercise in putting out good-sounding statements. Instead, it's a seizure of governmental lawmaking authority designed to make the government work on behalf of the majority, rather than continuing to serve as a colonized lackey for corporations.

Instead of diluting themselves to meet the needs of already-institutionalized groups who aren't going anywhere, the Occupy folks must move in the opposite direction: deepen and strengthen their effort by demanding structural change. That means moving away from the mainstream progressive organizations and the institutional advocacy they promote (which has proven ineffective against the type of consolidated wealth that influences decisions about every aspect of our lives today) and towards a new form of advocacy and activism. Rather than negotiating the terms of our de-occupation, we can and must rewrite the very rules under which our system operates.

Mainstream progressive groups have failed by working within legal and regulatory systems purposefully structured to subordinate communities to corporate power. Transformative movements don't operate that way. Abolitionists never sought to regulate the slave trade; they sought freedom and rights for slaves. Suffragists didn't seek concessions but demanded the right for all women to vote.

The Occupy movement must begin to use lawmaking activities in cities and towns to build a new legal structure of rights that empowers community majorities over corporate minorities, rather than the other way around.

It's taken a century's worth of manufactured and concocted legal doctrines to create an environment so skewed in the favor of corporations and their decision makers that not only our legislatures but also our courts can be wielded against us. Our country's wealth inequality did not arise overnight, but emerged slowly as the corporate minority eviscerated almost every memory of a true democratic system.

They've built a system that not only allows those with the most wealth to have the most decision-making power, but one in which our most essential constitutional rights have now been bestowed onto corporate "persons," thus insulating them from governing authority.

What's been happening in communities such as Pittsburgh and Spokane since the early 2000s is a revolution that takes those constitutional rights back and makes them work for communities again. Residents of over a hundred rural American communities have now seized their local governments by using municipal lawmaking power to recognize rights for nature, to strip corporations of certain claimed rights, and to elevate community decision-making rights above the claimed "rights" of corporations. In the process, they've stopped everything from proposed corporate factory farms to natural gas fracking and corporate water withdrawals.

These communities have begun to understand that the specific issues that affect them cannot be solved without dismantling a structure of law, government, and culture that guarantees that corporate minorities will continue to make decisions on energy, agriculture, and resource extraction.

Occupy Wall Street must become Occupy New York City—with groups of New Yorkers seizing the city and its boroughs and using the municipal entities to align their governing structures with their demands. That may mean eliminating corporate rights within the city, recognizing the rights of neighborhoods, and restoring labor rights within the workplace.

Occupy Seattle and Portland must actually occupy their municipalities via citizen initiatives and other processes to begin to change the law with which their cities operate by eliminating corporate rights and privileges.

This means understanding that our current system, in which a corporate minority wields a stranglehold over 99% of us, won't change just because one bill is introduced into congress, or promises are made by financial institutions. Structural change—focused on toppling the corporate domination of policy on everything from energy to transportation to finance—must be forced. We must begin in our cities and towns, then drive upwards against state and federal frameworks of law that protect decision-making authority by the 1%. In each of the cities where we live, we need to start working together to define the rights we need and then use our municipal structures to obtain them.

As winter nears, the Occupy movement should take note of community organizer Saul Alinsky's observation in *Rules for Radicals*, "A tactic that drags on too long becomes a drag." There may only be a brief window to convert street-level momentum into organized rights-legislating movements in each of our local communities.

Thomas Linzey is the executive director of the Community Environmental Legal Defense Fund. Jeff Reifman is co-founder of Envision Seattle, a freelance writer, and an organizer. This chapter first appeared on YesMagazine.org on October 14, 2011.

CHAPTER 14

GOING TO THE STREETS TO GET THINGS DONE

RALPH NADER

What took them so long—these jobless, poor, voiceless, excluded, defrauded, disrespected, fed up thousands, who are learning that half of what democracy means is showing up and staying—in this case—in the parks and the streets? Isn't that the lesson of American history?

The plutocrats of Wall Street and the oligarchs who serve them in Washington, DC, always sweat a little when people are in the streets. That is what happened during the drive to get women the right to vote, and the great challenges from organized demonstrators of farmers and workers in the latter half of the nineteenth century. Later it was the marches and rallies that sent the message of restraint and retreat to the bosses and launched the modern civil rights, women's rights, environmental, and peace movements.

Persistent street action breaks through the mass media's adhesion to status-quo definitions of news. It is unpredictable, visual, and flares when police overreact. It is hard to ignore, especially when the Internet is already actively reporting and commenting. Messages of resistance are coming from the indignation of engaged real people with real stories of injustice, deprivation, and moral outrage. These personal declarations, day after day, are harder to ignore than similar portrayals in the many muckraking books, magazines, and documentaries.

Being here, there, and everywhere in communities around the country exudes spontaneity and new energy. Mass media like spontaneity and new energy—people new to the causes that old-line groups have espoused more decorously for many years. (Our large presidential campaign rally in October 2008 in front of the New York Stock Exchange, during the crash, was largely ignored—except for an article in *The New York Times.*) There are times, places, and styles that produce sparks glowing with the potential to put more heat on an establishment unready for such grassroots perturbations.

Already, the Occupy encampments in small, mid-sized, and large towns—with a core still near Wall Street—have shown that the people have a pulse; that they have breaking points beyond which they will not remain passive.

The campers and the marchers are discovering that they have power—the crucial first stage of liberation from growing up powerless and under corporate domination—the two go together—into a process of self-realization. They are together finding talents and skills, temperaments and visions, resilience and determination that they may not have thought they had.

The Wall Street fat cats, in their private conversations, must have been wondering how a collapsed economy, the direct loss of eight million jobs, trillions of dollars in pensions and savings, and a taxpayer-funded bailout of the crooks and speculators who continue bad practices without remorse could persist without sustained protests by the victims. They now have the first stage of their answer.

We can be certain that the power structure is now analyzing the most effective ways of cooling down and drying up this decentralized, leaderless, growing occupation of the peoples' commons in scores of communities, with the "whole world watching" (to borrow a phrase from the 1960s). The corporate supremacists and their political allies will, of course, rely first on police power to clear the spaces and the tents. That will only serve to provoke even greater numbers of people to join the pioneers. What comes next is unknown, but it is most likely that a series of contingency plans are already on the drawing board to thwart a civic movement that shows signs of becoming very serious indeed.

Occupy Wall Street and its many supporters are already emboldening those in business, government, university, and union circles, who have been self-censoring, to take the next step to speak out and stand tall. This is what happened in the 1960s—first with civil rights and then with the anti-Vietnam war movements. They sparked other challenges that liberated minds, and long-repressed initiatives for change leading to legislation protecting consumers, the environment, and worker safety. In evaluating the Occupy challengers today, consider such penumbras that are exciting other efforts for justice that unite around the need to shift power from the few to the many along with the many resources that come with that dynamic.

Ralph Nader is a consumer advocate, lawyer, author, and former presidential candidate. His Web site is Nader.org.

CHAPTER 15

THE OCCUPATION OF HOPE:
LETTER TO A DEAD MAN

REBECCA SOLNIT

Dear young man who died on the fourth day of this turbulent 2011, dear Mohammed Bouazizi,

I want to write you about an astonishing year—with three months yet to run. I want to tell you about the power of despair and the margins of hope and the bonds of civil society.

I wish you could see the way that your small life and large death became a catalyst for the fall of so many dictators in what is known as the Arab Spring.

We are now in some sort of an American Fall. Civil society here has suddenly hit the ground running, and we are all headed toward a future no one imagined when you, a young Tunisian vegetable seller capable of giving so much, who instead had so much taken from you, burned yourself to death to protest your impoverished and humiliated state.

You lit yourself on fire on December 17, 2010, exactly nine months before Occupy Wall Street began. Your death two weeks later would be the beginning of so much. You lit yourself on fire because you were voiceless, powerless, and evidently without hope. And yet you must have had one small hope left: that your death would have an impact; that you, who had so few powers, even the power to make a decent living or protect your modest possessions or be treated fairly and decently by the police, had the power to protest. As it turned out, you had that power beyond your wildest dreams, and you had it because your hope, however diminished, was the dream of the many, the dream of what we now have started calling the 99%.

And so Tunisia erupted and overthrew its government, and Egypt caught fire, as did Bahrain, Syria, Yemen, and Libya, where the nonviolent protests elsewhere inspired a civil war the rebels have won after several bloody months. Who could have imagined a Middle East without Ben Ali of Tunisia, without Mubarak, without Gaddafi? And yet here we are, in the unimaginable world. Again. And almost everywhere.

Distinctively, in so many of these uprisings the participants were not advocating for one party or a simple position, but for a better world, for dignity, for respect, for real democracy, for belonging, for hope and possibility—and their economic underpinnings. The Spanish young whose future had been sold out to benefit corporations and who were nicknamed the *Indignados*, lived in the plazas of Spain this summer. Occupied Madrid, like occupied Tahrir Square, preceded Occupy Wall Street. The United States had one great eruption in Wisconsin this winter, when the citizenry occupied their state capitol building in Madison for weeks. Now the Occupy movement has spilled over from Wall Street. Hundreds of occupations are happening all over North America: in Oklahoma City and Tijuana, in Victoria and Fort Lauderdale.

The 99%

"We are the 99%" is the cry of the Occupy movement. This summer, one of the flyers that helped launch the Occupy Wall Street protest read: "We, the 99%, call for an open general assembly August 9, 7:30 p.m. at the Potato Famine Memorial, NYC." It was an assembly to discuss the September 17 occupation to come.

The Irish Hunger Memorial, so close to Wall Street, commemorates the million Irish peasants who starved in the 1840s, while Ireland remained a food-exporting country and the landed gentry continued to profit. It's a monument to the exploitation of the many by the few, to the forces that turned some of our ancestors—including my mother's four Irish grandparents—into immigrants, forces that are still pushing people out of farms, homes, nations, and regions. The Irish famine was one of the great examples of those disasters of the modern era that are not crises of scarcity, but of distribution. The United States is now the wealthiest country the world has ever known, and has an abundance of natural resources, as well as of nurses, doctors, universities, teachers, housing, and food—so ours, too, is a crisis of distribution. Everyone could have everything they need and the rich would still be rich enough, but you know that *enough* isn't a concept for them. They're greedy, and their thirty-year grab for more has carved away at what's minimally necessary for the survival and dignity of the rest of us. So the Famine Memorial couldn't have been a more appropriate place for Occupy Wall Street to begin.

Later in August came the Web site started by a twenty-eight-year-old New York City activist, "We Are the 99%," to which hundreds daily now submit photographs of themselves. Each of them also testifies to the bleak conditions they find themselves in. It's a Web site of unremitting waking nightmares, economic bad dreams that a little wealth redistribution would eliminate (even without eliminating the wealthy). The people contributing aren't asking for luxuries. They would simply prefer not to be worked to death like so many nineteenth century millworkers, nor to have their whole world come crashing down if they get sick. They want to survive with dignity, and their testimonies will break your heart.

"We are not goods in the hands of politicians and bankers," was the slogan of the first student protest called in Spain this year. Your beautiful generation, Mohammed Bouazizi, has arisen and is bringing the rest of us along, even here in the United States.

What is Your Occupation?

Occupy Wall Street. Occupy together. Occupy New Orleans, Portland, Stockton, Boston, Las Cruces, Minneapolis. Occupy. The very word is a manifesto, a position statement, and a position as well. For so many people, their occupation is their identity, and when a job is lost, they become not just unemployed, but no one. The Occupy movement offers them a new occupation, work that won't pay the bills, but a job worth doing. "Lost my job, found an occupation," said one sign in the crowd of witty signs.

There is, of course, a bleaker meaning for the word occupation, as in, "the United States is occupying Iraq." Even National Public Radio gives the Dow Jones report several times a day, as though the rise and fall of the stock market had not long ago been decoupled from the rise and fall of genuine measures of well-being for the 99%. A small part of Wall Street, which has long occupied us as if it were a foreign power, is now occupied as though it were a foreign country.

Wall Street *is* a foreign country—and maybe an enemy country as well. And now it's occupied. The way that Native Americans occupied Alcatraz Island in San Francisco Bay for eighteen months four decades ago and galvanized a national Native American rights movement. You pick someplace to stand, and when you stand there, you find your other occupation, as a member of civil society. At this moment in history, occupation should be everyone's occupation.

Baby Pictures of a Revolt

Young man whose despair gave birth to hope, no one knows what the future holds. When you set yourself afire almost ten months ago, you certainly didn't know, nor do any of us know now, what the long-term outcome of the Arab Spring will be, let alone this American Fall. Such a movement arrives in the world like a newborn. Who knows its fate, or even whether it will survive to grow up? Zuccotti Park is just two blocks from Wall Street, and also just a block from Ground Zero, the site of the 9/11 attacks. On that day, it was badly damaged. September 21, my dear friend Marina Sitrin wrote me from Occupy Wall Street: "There are people from more diverse backgrounds racially, more diverse age groups, including not just a few children here with their parents, and a number of working people from the area. In particular, some of the security guards from the 9/11 memorial a block away have been coming by for lunch and chatting with people, as has a local group of construction workers."

If the Arab Spring was the decade-later antithesis of 9/11, a largely nonviolent, publicly inclusive revolt that forced the Western world to get over its fearful fantasy that all young Muslims are terrorists, jihadis, and suicide bombers, then Occupy Wall Street, which began six days after the tenth anniversary of that nightmarish day in September, is the other half of 9/11 in New York. What was remarkable about that day ten years ago is how calmly and beautifully everyone behaved. New Yorkers helped each other down those dozens of flights of stairs in the Twin Towers and away from the catastrophe, while others lined up to give blood, desperate to do something, anything, to participate, to be part of a newfound sense of community that arose in the city that day.

When I began to study the history of urban disaster years ago, I found such unexpected exhibitions of that kind of joy again and again, uniting the generative moments of protests, demonstrations, revolts, and revolutions with the aftermath of some disasters. Even when the losses were terrible, the ways that people came together to meet the occasion were almost always inspiring.

Since I wrote *A Paradise Built in Hell: The Extraordinary Communities That Arise in Disaster*, I have been asked again and again whether economic crisis begets the same kind of community as sudden disasters. It did in Argentina in 2001, when the economy crashed there. And it has now, in the streets of New York and many other cities, in 2011. A sign at Occupy San Francisco said, "IT'S TIME." It is. It's been time for a long time.

No Hope But in Ourselves

Our economy collapsed three years ago this month to headlines like "Capitalism is dead" in the business press. There was certainly some fury and outrage at the time, but the real reaction was delayed, or decoyed. The outrage of the moment did, in fact, result in a powerful grassroots movement that focused on a single political candidate to fix it all for us, as he promised he would. It was a beautiful movement, a hopeful movement, much more so than its candidate. The movement got its lone candidate into the highest office in the land, where he remains today, and then walked away as though the job was done. It had just begun.

That movement could have fought the corporations, given us a real climate-change policy, and more, but it allowed itself to be disbanded as though one elected politician were the equivalent of ten million citizens, of civil society itself. It was a broad-based movement, of all ages and races, and I think it's back, disillusioned with politicians and electoral politics, determined this time to do it for itself, beyond and outside the corroded arenas of institutional power.

I don't know exactly who this baby looks like, but I know that who you look like is not who you will become. This unanticipated baby has a month behind it and a future ahead of it that none of us can see, but its birth should give you hope.

Love,

Rebecca

Rebecca Solnit is the author of thirteen books, including A Paradise Built in Hell: The Extraordinary Communities That Arise in Disaster *and* Hope in the Dark: Untold Histories, Wild Possibilities. *She is also a regular contributor to TomDispatch.com, where this chapter first appeared on October 18, 2011.*

CHAPTER 16

TEN WAYS TO SUPPORT THE OCCUPY MOVEMENT

SARAH VAN GELDER

How can you help build the power of the Occupy movement?
Here are some places to start:

1. Show up at the occupied space near you.
Find a location near you at www.occupytogether.org. See if they have a Facebook page. Bring a tent or tarp to stay. Or just stop by to talk to people, participate in a general assembly, hold a sign, or help serve food.

2. Start your own occupation.
Call together friends and acquaintances. Reach out to people you don't normally work with so you can better represent the 99%. Talk together about what you want to occupy, and why.

3. Support those who are occupying.
Most sites need food, warm clothes, blankets, tarps, sleeping bags, communications gear, and money. Search #needsofthe-occupiers on Twitter for real time updates or check in with your local occupiers.

4. Get into the debates and the teach-ins.
Many occupation sites have workshops and discussions on the critical issues of our time. Get into the discussion. Bring copies of this book, *YES! Magazine*, or other materials to share. Listen to perspectives you haven't heard before, and share your own.

5. Tell your story.
Post your story of being part of the 99% on Facebook, Twitter, blogs, or in letters to the editor. When you share, others see that they aren't alone. Community plus insight makes us powerful.

6. Be the media.
Bring your video recorder, camera phone, or laptop and report on the occupation. Highlight the human dimension of the protests. Show the faces of those involved.

7. Name the meaning of this moment.
What will make the world better for the 99%? Speak out on the issue that means the most to you. Include the phrase, "I am the 99%."

8. Insist that public officials treat the occupations with respect.
The eviction of the Zuccotti Park occupiers on Wall Street was averted by massive public resistance. After a huge public outcry, the mayor of Oakland apologized for a brutal police assault that left an Iraq war veteran in critical condition. Other occupations need support. Ask your local officials to respect the right to assemble of the 99%.

9. Study and teach nonviolent techniques.
Violence can badly damage the movement. Learn how to lovingly and firmly interrupt and contain violence, and teach what you know.

10. Be resilient.
This movement must last for the long term. Don't get disillusioned. The demand for a society that serves the 99% won't go away. Help the movement evolve.

The genie is out of the bottle. People will no longer accept the systematic transfer of wealth and power from the 99% to the 1%. In this remarkable, leaderless movement, each one of the 99% who gets involved helps shape history.

Sarah van Gelder is co-founder and executive editor of YES! Magazine.

YES! is an award-winning, nonprofit, national media organization that supports people's active engagement in solving today's social, political, economic, and environmental challenges.

Powerful Ideas, Practical Actions

Online and in print, *YES!* shows how we can create a world that works for the 99%, not just the 1%. We outline a path forward with in-depth analysis, tools for citizen engagement, and stories about real people working for a better world.

Subscribe to *YES!* Magazine

Each issue of *YES!* Magazine focuses on a specific theme—such as how to solve the jobs crisis and respect the planet at the same time, who is doing the best work to reduce global warming, what science tells us about how to be happy, how the people can take back control of democracy.

Published quarterly and printed on 100% postconsumer waste paper, *YES!* features powerful ideas from today's most compelling thought leaders, including Wendell Berry, Bill McKibben, Frances Moore Lappé, David Korten, Annie Leonard, Van Jones, Vandana Shiva, Parker Palmer, Winona LaDuke, and David Sirota.

Subscribe at YesMagazine.org or call (800) 937-4451

Visit our Web site: YesMagazine.org

With daily posts, *YES!* provides a "*YES!* take" on headline news, keeping up with emerging social movements and showing positive possibilities the mainstream media miss. Features include articles and blogs, photo essays, audio and video, and a searchable archive of thousands of stories. Our articles are available for free and licensed under the Creative Commons.

Sign up for *YES!* This Week

Our free weekly newsletter rounds up our top stories of the week. Readers tell us it lifts their spirits and spurs their imagination about the world we can create together.

Sign up at YesMagazine.org/SignUp

Follow *YES!* on Facebook and Twitter

We post stories on Facebook and tweet every day to keep our fans and followers up on current news, events, and opportunities for engagement.

facebook.com/yesmagazine Twitter handle: @yesmagazine

DISCOVER A DIFFERENT STORY.

YES! goes beyond the day's problems to spotlight solutions for a better world.

•

YES! forecasts major trends and introduces emerging leaders years before they appear in conventional media.

•

YES! features powerful examples of what's working and offers tools for taking action.

Berrett-Koehler Books for the 99%

Berrett-Koehler Publishers is a community dedicated to creating a world that works for all. We're committed to publishing books that challenge the underlying beliefs, mindsets, institutions, and structures that keep generating the same cycles of problems, no matter who our leaders are or what improvement programs they adopt. Below we list some of our books that we think would be of particular interest to readers of *This Changes Everything*. But we encourage you to go our website (www.bkconnection.com) and look around for yourself!

David C. Korten
Agenda for a New Economy: From Phantom Wealth to Real Wealth, 2nd Edition
Paperback, 336 pages, ISBN 978-1-60509-375-8
PDF ebook, ISBN 978-1-60509-376-5

When Corporations Rule the World, 2nd Edition
Paperback, 400 pages, ISBN 978-1-887208-04-8

Jeffrey D. Clements
Corporations Are Not People: Why They Have More Rights Than You Do and What You Can Do About It
Paperback, 240 pages, ISBN 978-1-60994-105-5
PDF ebook, ISBN 978-1-60994-106-2

Thom Hartmann
The Thom Hartmann Reader
Paperback, 360 pages, ISBN 978-1-57675-761-1
PDF ebook, ISBN 978-1-60994-559-6

Unequal Protection: How Corporations Became "People"—and How You Can Fight Back, 2nd Edition
Paperback, 384 pages, ISBN 978-1-60509-559-2
PDF ebook, ISBN 978-1-60509-560-8

Rebooting the American Dream: 11 Ways to Rebuild Our Country
Paperback, 240 pages, ISBN 978-1-60994-029-4
PDF ebook, ISBN 978-1-60509-909-5

Brian Miller and Mike Lapham
The Self-Made Myth: And the Truth About How Government Helps Individuals and Businesses Succeed
Paperback, 216 pages, ISBN 978-1-60994-506-0
PDF ebook, ISBN 978-1-60994-507-7

Margaret Wheatley and Deborah Frieze
Walk Out Walk On: A Learning Journey into Communities Daring to Live the Future Now
Paperback, 288 pages, ISBN 978-1-60509-731-2
PDF ebook, ISBN 978-1-60509-732-9

John Perkins
Confessions of an Economic Hit Man
Hardcover, 280 pages, ISBN 978-1-57675-301-9
PDF ebook, ISBN 978-1-57675-512-9

Deanna Zandt
Share This! How You Will Change the World with Social Networking
Paperback, 192 pages, ISBN 978-1-60509-416-8
PDF ebook, ISBN 978-1-60509-417-5

Linda Stout
Collective Visioning: How Groups Can Work Together for a Just and Sustainable Future
Paperback, 216 pages, ISBN 978-1-60509-882-1
PDF ebook, ISBN 978-1-60509-883-8

Marjorie Kelly
The Divine Right of Capital: Dethroning the Corporate Aristocracy
Paperback, 288 pages, ISBN 978-1-57675-237-1
PDF ebook, ISBN 978-1-60994-194-9

John Cavanagh and Jerry Mander, Editors
Alternatives to Economic Globalization: A Better World Is Possible, 2nd Edition
Paperback, 432 pages, ISBN 978-1-57675-303-3
PDF ebook, ISBN 978-1-60509-409-0

John de Graaf, David Wann, and Thomas H. Naylor
Affluenza: The All-Consuming Epidemic, 2nd Edition
Paperback, 312 pages, ISBN 978-1-57675-357-6
PDF ebook, ISBN 978-1-60509-647-6

John McKnight and Peter Block
The Abundant Community: Awakening the Power of Families and Neighborhoods
Paperback, 192 pages, ISBN 978-1-60994-081-2
PDF ebook, ISBN 978-1-60509-626-1

BK® Berrett–Koehler Publishers, Inc.
San Francisco, *www.bkconnection.com*

800.929.2929

MIX
From responsible sources
FSC
www.fsc.org FSC® C004691